The Cold-and-Hunger Dance

The Cold-and-Hunger Dance

☙

DIANE GLANCY

UNIVERSITY OF NEBRASKA PRESS   *Lincoln ✷ London*

⊗ The paper in this book meets the minimum
requirements of American National Standard for
Information Sciences — Permanence of Paper for
Printed Library Materials, ANSI Z39.48-1984.

Selections reprinted from *Black Elk Speaks*, by
John G. Neihardt, appear by permission of the
University of Nebraska Press. Copyright 1932,
1959, 1972, by John G. Neihardt. Copyright ©
1961 by the John G. Neihardt Trust.
Selections reprinted from *The Sacred Pipe*, by
Joseph Epes Brown, appear by permission of the
University of Oklahoma Press. Copyright © 1953, 1989
by the University of Oklahoma Press, Norman,
Publishing Division of the University.

Library of Congress Cataloging-in-Publication Data
Glancy, Diane.
The cold-and-hunger dance / Diane Glancy.
p.   cm.
Includes bibliographical references.
ISBN 0-8032-2173-8 (hardcover : alk. paper)
1. Glancy, Diane — Biography.   2. Women authors,
American — 20th century — Biography.   3. Indians of
North America — Social life and customs.   I. Title.
PS3557.L294Z464   1998   818'.5409 — dc21   [B]   98-11407   CIP

Contents

Acknowledgments

Acknowledgment to the following anthologies and journals for publications:

Contemporary Author's Autobiography Series, vol. 24 (1997), for "The Cold-and-Hunger Dance"

Women/Writing/Teaching: An Anthology of Women's Voices, edited by Jan Zlotnik Schmidt (Albany: SUNY Press, © 1998, All Rights Reserved), for "She-ro-ism," by permission of the publisher

XCP / Cross Cultural Poetics, vol. 1 (1997), for "*nahna adulvdi gesvi* (of that wanting which is)"

Native American Religious Identity in a Post-Christian Age: Unforgotten Gods, edited by Jace Weaver (Maryknoll NY: Orbis Books, 1998), for "Sun Dance"

Literacy Matters: Reading and Writing in the Second Wave of Multiculturalism, edited by Lillian Bridwell-Bowles (Upper Saddle River NJ: Prentice-Hall, Inc., 1998), and *Colors: Minnesota's Journal of Opinion and the Arts by Writers of Color*, vol. 3 (May–June 1994), for "The Bible and *Black Elk Speaks*"

American Letters & Commentary, no. 10 (1998), for "Photography"

Chain: A Journal of Experimental Languages, Different Languages Issue (1998), for "A Fieldbook of Textual Migrations"

Acknowledgment to organizations for grants and fellowships:

The Jerome Foundation for a 1995 travel grant that made "Sun Dance" possible

The Frances Allen Fellowship, Newberry Library, Chicago

A 1995 Master Fellowship from the Lannan Foundation, the Fine Arts Work Center, Provincetown, Massachusetts

A 1995 Wallace Sabbatical grant from Macalester College

The Minnesota Private College Research Foundation, with funds provided by the Blandin Foundation of Grand Rapids, Minnesota, for supporting a project during which a part of "North Shore Portrait" was written

"On Boards and Broken Pieces of the Ship" was first presented as a lecture in a History of God seminar at Macalester College

"A Fieldbook of Textual Migrations" was presented at the 1997 Cross Cultural Poetics conference at the University of Minnesota

We found our horses and rode back to the railroad, the Messiah flying along in the air with us and teaching us the songs for the new dances. At the railroad he left us and told us to return to our people, and tell them, and all the people of the red nations, what we had seen; and he promised us that he would return to the clouds no more, but would remain at the end of the earth and lead the ghosts of our fathers to meet us when the next winter passed. — KICKING BEAR, 1890

The Cold-and-Hunger Dance

Eggs

I've got wooden eggs in a wire hen hanging in my kitchen. One egg, from Germany, has a few letters of the alphabet on it. It was designed by a group of Gypsy women because they were losing their language.

I have a speckled egg, an egg with dalmatian spots, a cedar egg, an Italian glass egg from Venice, a Russian egg, an Easter egg, a carnelian Chinese egg with a carved design.

The yard is full of trees. The wire hen is full of eggs. Stoic eggs. Eggs of faith. I have a geometric beaded egg from a Peyote culture, the beads held with beeswax. Jagged reds and greens as trees in the yard. As old gasoline pumps. The trees step out of fields. The cows and crops move over.

There is a blue reindeer with jags of lightning.

My spurs jangle as I pump gas.

I am a marginal voice in several worlds. I can tell several stories at once. Mixed-blood stories of academic life and the experience of Christianity. Nothing fitting with anything else. The word *community* has always meant *being left out*. But in the cold-and-hunger dance, the voice is one story holding the disparate parts.

The Cold-and-Hunger Dance

. . . therefore I set my face like a flint —Isaiah 50:7

I had a hunger for words. The house I lived in as a child was quiet. I was quiet. I was three before I had a sibling. My mother handled the words. I wanted someone to listen. I wanted someone to talk to.

I wanted my own voice forming my will.

I wanted books. The fortified cities of them. I wanted to be a maker of those fortifications. A fortifier. Because my parents are gone and they were once young and sturdy. Though they also tore down. And were torn down.

I was born between two cultures. My father was Cherokee. My mother, English and German. But we weren't Cherokee enough to be accepted as Indian, nor was I white enough to be accepted as white. I could walk in both worlds; I could walk in neither. I lived in a no man's land. A no man's land that moved.

My father worked for the stockyards in Kansas City. He was transferred several times. I went to several schools in the Midwest. Frances Willard in Kansas City. Flackville in Indianapolis. Normandy in St. Louis. I graduated from the University of Missouri in 1964, from University of Central Oklahoma in 1983, and from the University of Iowa Writer's Workshop in 1988. I have been at Macalester College in St. Paul, Minnesota, since then. I write and teach Native American Literature and creative writing in its many forms: poetry, fiction, creative nonfiction, scriptwriting.

I've always wanted to tell stories, to tell them in my own way. According to oral tradition, I could speak with the trail of voices. I could talk with my own voice, and the way of my words could change the structure of the story. I could speak indirectly if I wanted: talking about one thing while meaning another.

The Judeo-Christian heritage, which is full of stories of expanding boundaries, and church, where I heard those stories, have been a part of my middle-class life also. I think I am a Christian because of the words in the Bible. The sturdiness of them. The *oratures* of them.

> He stretches the north over the empty place, and hangs the earth upon nothing. (Job 26:7)

> He binds up the waters in his thick clouds; and the cloud is not torn under them. (Job 26:8)

> He has set a bound that the waves may not pass over, that they turn not again to cover the earth. (Psalms 104:9)

> Will you not tremble at my presence, who has placed the sand for the bound of the sea; and though its waves toss themselves, yet can they not prevail; though they roar, they cannot pass over. (Jeremiah 5:22)

I felt an *unformedness* I wanted form for. Or maybe I wanted boundaries for. It was through words. The stories of them. Their *storyness*. It was the Word God held out as a pole for me to take hold of.

There is something in the Bible. A relativity of *changeableness*, yet an absolute dry-ground in the flood. The waves could come so far, but no farther. Jesus was a construct of voice and a centering in the turmoil I felt.

My father had come from northern Arkansas where his white father had been a country doctor and his mother, a Cherokee woman, his third wife. My father's religion was not in the Cherokee traditon, but came in the form of church.

My father liked to travel. From Kansas City, we made trips to my grandparents' farm in Kansas and my father's mother in Viola, Arkansas. We went to California to visit my Aunt Helen, and to Itasca State Park in Minnesota. When we lived in Indiana, we went to Lake Michigan and the sand dunes, Turkey Run State Park, and Washington DC, Jamestown, and Williamsburg. When we lived in St. Louis, we made trips to Florida and to the Lake of the Ozarks in Missouri where Aunt Mil and Uncle Carl had a cabin.

I remember feeling limits as a child, but when I look at the photo album, there was also migration.

When I was eight or nine, I had to take swimming lessons at Paseo High School in Kansas City. I still have an image of that pool. The shape of it, shallow on one end, deep on the other, something like the state of Oklahoma without its panhandle, where I lived much of my adult life. The weight of it filled with water. I was underwater swimming for the surface. I could see light. I swam toward it. When I think back on those early years, it was my father who was the light. My Aunt Mil in her saddle shoes was the one who held out the pole. Because she was never angry with me.

I never did learn to swim.

It was an overwhelming experience that stands as a defining image of my childhood.

That swimming pool is still in my head. I drain it with my writing. My mother's unhappiness as a mother. Her disapproval of me. Whether it was my darkness intruding upon her or something disagreeable in me, we had conflict.

But that point of fear and drowning is the undercurrent of my writing.

Words are a netting, a surface of waves, that disrupt the joint of process. Wind patterns on the lake. Interrelated and touching one another. Though it seems they don't. I feel the frustration of words in their bondage of having to explain.

A swimming pool full of waves. That was my adolescence.

> He had seven sons and three daughters . . . And their father gave
> them inheritance among their brethren. (Job 42:13–15.)

Though I felt I was nothing, I knew I had an inheritance. I struggled through self-devaluation and fear and inferiority and isolation. There was a steel wire that ran through my life. Wherever it came from. A combination of several sources, probably. Self-will and determination.

An aunt without children who approved of me. A house with two parents that remained whole though broken. The words from the Bible.

He hath compassed the water with a boundary. (Job 26:10)

When I write a story, I feel those variables moving in different patterns. I think it's why I write in several genres. Imagination moves across the landscape and enters the text, and takes part in forming the creative act, which unites my fragments in a loose bonding, which moves to other bondings of other fragments and makes sources-of-energy spots.

Writing is the creating of a *source structure*.

In wording and naming the act of living, in shaping shapelessness, a determination, a determinacy, speaks a continuum of will and fortitude and not giving up.

When my work was rejected, I kept writing. And the manuscripts piled up. I sent them out, received them back, sent them out again. The title of my second collection of drama, *Cargo*, probably came from carrying all those words around.

Now that I'm older, I think, looking back, what it was to live my life. It was long ago and I wanted to write and when my two children napped, I wrote. I had a file cabinet, and then I bought another to hold what I had written. I moved it with me, from Oklahoma to Iowa to Minnesota, and twice since I've lived in Minnesota.

Words are a dynamic of self seeking connection.

Waves cropping a lake.

A lake cropping its waves.

Words are the reflection of water in the pool of the eye.

A place I was looking for made of images of meaning.

A more-than-one on which to focus.

A flag in the wind.

Someone speaking from far way.

I can see the mouth move.

I see it like a flag in the wind.

There is a crosspool of floodings in the complexities of current.

There is a voice saying, "hold on, it will connect and *go somewhere*," in a broken surface on which words spread into many genres.

From 1964 to 1983, I was married. The image I have from those years was a dream I had once, early in the marriage. I was trying to drive a loaded 18-wheeler up a sandy incline.

Those were the years I began writing.

I also wanted to return to school. After I got my B.A. at the University of Missouri, it was twenty years before I continued my education. My years as an undergraduate had been unsettled. Insecure. I couldn't study. I didn't think I could. My grades suffered.

The turmoil of my life still circled. Everything fell back on me. I worked with poetry and then story. I worked with creative nonfiction, drama, and the novel. It wasn't until 1984 that I had anything published.

Two early novels, *The Only Piece of Furniture in the House* and *Fuller Man*, written during my marriage, weren't published for fifteen years. I began *Monkey Secret*, my third collection of short stories, as an undergraduate at the University of Missouri. I remember writing one of the sections, "The Wooden Tub," in my first creative writing class. It was nearly thirty years before the other parts of the story were finished and published.

My historical novel, *Pushing the Bear*, about the 1838 Trail of Tears, the removal of 13,000 Cherokees from the southeast to Indian Territory, took nearly eighteen years to write. Over the years, the many voices in the novel came to my imagination during research or travel. Or sometimes when I was doing something else, there would be Maritole or Knobowtee. It's where I heard them anyway, in the imagination. A series of voices, a story of many voices walking the trail, telling their side of it.

When I was in New York, I visited the Smithsonian Museum of the American Indian in the Custom House. I saw a Seminole robe that was a patchwork of color and geometric design. I thought of my novel as a patterning of voices with dialogue and conflicts unfolding in relationship to one another. When I saw a northwestern tribe "button blanket," I thought of my novel as a "voice blanket." My grandmother on my mother's side made quilts. Maybe in sewing the scattered voices together in the novel, I'm doing what she did, only in a different way.

I also thought of *Pushing the Bear* as the noise of voices after their sound has stopped.

The title came to me when I was at the Gilcrease Museum in Tulsa, down among the shelves in the storage rooms. I saw a small ivory statue of an Eskimo man pushing the rump of a bear. *Pushing the Bear* came immediately to mind.

Sometimes my writing comes quicky. *Flutie* was written during my 1995–96 sabbatical year. It's the story of a young woman who is shy and cannot speak, but through circumstance and ceremony and an act of the will, she finds her voice and speaks. I made two trips back to Oklahoma to hear the characters and the land.

I'm glad each piece comes in its own way. Writing is a continuous process, changing as it goes.

I have the title for a new novel, *An American Language*. I was thinking about our American language when I was traveling in Germany recently. I said that I felt limited when I traveled because I only had one language. But someone said, "It's the right one."

At the conference in Munich, I was talking about the experimentation I liked to do with the American language. I talked about the possibilities of changing syntax. The possibilities for opening the language to accommodate minority and women's voices. How in not having ownership over language, it expands to do what you want to do as a writer. The Germans said that the German language didn't have that capacity. If you changed a word in German, or tried to stretch it, you'd feel that something was wrong.

Maybe our language is more fluid. Elastic. It's what I want language to be, anyway.

It's also what I want genres to be. I think it's why I began experimenting with the short story collections I wrote. My first two short fiction books, *Trigger Dance* and *Firesticks*, were written in Oklahoma where I was living with my husband and children. They contain first-person narratives and short-short fiction pieces as well as traditional short stories. *Firesticks* begins with a story about Louis, a colorblind young man who tries to imagine color. The book continues with a personal essay, then a poetic piece about a truck driver, and then the first section of the title piece, "Firesticks." Then there's another personal-voice piece and another chapter of "Firesticks." Then more stories and personal-voice pieces with more parts of "Firesticks" woven between them. I think I wrote the book that way because I felt the fragmentation of my own life, and of my father's heritage, in the breaking up of a solid place.

I've already mentioned *Monkey Secret*, my third collection. It is also a broken-voice piece. The book is three short stories followed by the novella "Monkey Secret." That monkeys were once men was an idea I got from the *Popol Vuh*, the Mayan council book.

On the jacket flap, the editor, Reginald Gibbons, writes:

> These tales of Native American life explore the essential American territory, the border-between: between past and present, between native and immigrant cultures, between self and society.
>
> The short novel, *Monkey Secret,* combines traditional Native American storytelling and contemporary narrative techniques to explore the coming of age of a young girl of mixed race and heritage in rural northern Arkansas. Jean Pierce narrates her passage from childhood to maturity with typically Native American circularity and digression. Each chapter of *Monkey Secret* is like a single perfect bead on a string; Jean's impressionistic vignettes growing up with her extended family at their farm in Haran, Arkansas, spending summers at the cabin on Bull Shoals Lake, departing for college and returning to find her mother dying are threaded with the twin strands of her complex culture and her desperate love for her cousin Cedric.
>
> In its gaps and hesitations, the qualifications of thought and feeling, the meditative self-reflexiveness, this story interrogates narrative form while revealing the individuality and authenticity of the characters.

I had wanted to call the novella "Portrait of an Artist as a Young Woman," but I knew I couldn't get into those waters. It's about a young woman who lives in the crevice between the Christian world of her father and the mythic Cherokee world of her mother, who uses words to bridge the two irreconcilable worlds that were always moving apart from one another. One of the sections in the novella, however, is called "Sketches of an Artist as a Young Woman." I remember visiting Bull Shoals Lake in Arkansas when we went to see my father's mother. I remember being in a rowboat on *big* water. I also used the experiences I had at my Uncle Cari's cabin on the Lake of the Ozarks.

Creative nonfiction is a genre with a moving definition: memoir, autobiography, diary writing, journal keeping, travel pieces, essays on various subjects, book reviews, interviews, assemblages of personal experiences and reflections, experimentation with the variables of composition, and a combination of these different parts.

Claiming Breath and *The West Pole* are collections of creative nonfiction, combining lectures and book reviews with personal essays and fragmented prose pieces, all the while moving between traditional and disconnected writing styles, shifting the text, breaking into the sentence structure. Expanding the boundaries. Somehow communicating the ideas.

Native American storying is an act of *gathering* many voices to tell a story in many different ways. One voice alone is not enough because we are what we are in relationship to others, and we each have our different way of seeing. Native American writing is also an alignment of voices so the story comes through. A *relational stance* is the construct of the writing. In my short stories, poems, and creative nonfiction, I can follow the rules of conflict/resolution, one point of view, plot, and the usual, but there is something essential in Native storying that is not included, a migratory and interactive process of the moveable parts within the story. It's also the element of Native American oral tradition told with what it is not — the written word — then returned to what it is by the act of the voice. There's not a name for it in the genre field, but I'm trying to give solid nomenclature to something that is a moving process, and resists naming, other than a new oral tradition.

I think writing exists, in part, for healing, not only in the writer, but also for the reader/hearer. For instance, in Navajo sand paintings, the painter aligns the design in the sand to the hurt in the one needing healing, and the alignment draws the hurt into the painting, and then the painting is destroyed and the ailment along with it. Storying should do the same. It is much needed in a culture with a high alcoholism rate, poverty, and a struggle for racial esteem.

America is taking out of the melting pot what didn't melt: our voices and styles of storying. We are a fractured, pluralistic society, which our art should reflect. I think understanding cultures is the byword for our society. It seems to me art is the medium for understanding not only the differences between cultures, but within cultures as well. There is a vast difference between the Plains Indian and the Woodland cultures.

Sometimes, in the long cold of a Minnesota winter, I think about my writing. Especially when I'm chopping ice that's several inches thick on my sidewalk. Especially when I'm shoveling snow. The last storm, my snow shovel froze in a mound of old snow where I'd jabbed it. I had to shovel with a shovel with a broken handle.

At night when the ice on the roof shifts, the house moans and knocks with stories.

Over the years, I have written because I was hungry for words.

I have written because I was cold.

I think I've waited my whole life to teach, travel, and read my poetry and fiction in bookstores and at conferences.

Like my father, I want to be on the road. The fall of my sabbatical after receiving tenure, when I had a fellowship at the Provincetown Art Center in Massachusetts, I drove from St. Paul to the other side of Cleveland the first day. And from the other side of Cleveland to Provincetown. 1,465 miles in two days.

There was something I had to get through. Maybe like a piece of writing.

There were names I found like Ashtabula County in Ohio I had to get down.

And there were the trucks — *Yellow Transit. National Carriers. Transcontinental Registered Lines. Roadway. Consolidated Freight. Wells Fargo. J B Hunt. North American. Burlington. Falcon. Tuscarora. Mayflower.*

Some without names.

The turnpikes east of Wisconsin are walled cities. I felt locked on the highway with the truckers. But I was away from classes and department and committee meetings and grading papers.

There were seven tollgates through Chicago alone where I waited in the exhaust of their dust.

After two days by myself on the road, weary and spaced, my sense of identity, which is tied to place, also was in transit. I was one of those nameless trucks floating over the road. Disconnected. But in the movement of my car was place, I remembered. Migration was a state.

And I was in the walled city of my car.

If I could be from anywhere, it would be Ashtabula. If I could be with anyone, it would be one of those truckers. Those wedding-cake grooms up there decorated with lights. I would follow his truck across the Atlantic, if there were a highway there.

My children are grown and my relatives are gone, and I am with my words now.

Water I can't swim.

Water you are blank as I am.

Water you can swim.

Water you can hold me up.

Sometimes I think of my father who left his rural Cherokee heritage to be a real American — a boy scout leader — a provider for his family. I remember the hollowness and anger in him because he had a blank place where heritage should have been.

But I had a doll cart with two wheels my father made, and I'd pull my two dolls to a weeded lot by my house and play there all day mashing berries for food, playing out what was in my imagination. There was a life of the mind in which there was the making of metaphor, a development and insight into the relationship of parts — the likeness of differences — the difference of likenesses — the connectives and disconnectives — the making of something. I think I continue pushing my doll cart to the woods with my writing.

Because I didn't have music or mathematics or science — I made analogies. I made stories. But the principles of discovery and relationships may be the same.

The language of the imagination has the function to talk through connections that underlie things. I am in a relationship to something outside myself. I have a connection to words, and as I work, they connect with something larger.

I feel the variability. The layering of expanding thought processes, the opportunities, the options, the embellishment and elaborations. I generate my own life in the development of thought through words.

I have a reliable construction of change and the unexpected. I have a gist of certainty. My writing is a generator. A source of something — of words — of reasoning —

They brought me to the place where I am now. It's a full life full of ordinariness, really. I had nearly twenty years as a wife and mother. I've been divorced over fourteen. My children are on their own in different cities. This was a time dreaded by my mother's generation in the fifties. What do you do after the children are gone? Who are you outside your husband and family?

Those years with my children were meaningful — and I miss them sometimes. But now I get up in the morning and have coffee and read the newspaper and go to my word processor and go through my thoughts, and go back through them, and find that road into what I am saying. I guess it's always been Main Street under the elms.

I remember the decency of my parents despite their problems and economic straits — the unfairness they knew. My mother as a woman. My father as a man who had to live without part of himself. I remember the disillusionment, the boredom, I guess, of their marriage. The tediousness of life we all know. My anger at them —

But the carcasses of cattle hanged upside-down in the stockyards where my father worked, and Christ hanged rightside-up on his cross in church. There was faith in the blood-shed of Christ for the atonement of our shortcomings and sins. Christianity as a strained metaphor, so to speak. A thought process that links. Something like sand, which can be a boundary of the sea and a conduit of healing in a painting.

I have my own life now. I have a small house in St. Paul. When it's twenty below or when there's twenty inches of snow in one afternoon, my brother calls from Missouri and asks what I'm doing there. But I can shovel my walk and mow the lawn and reach the windows when I wash them. I have a sense of self in my thinking, which is an internal landscape. There are elements in the world that could wipe me out, but I have a heritage of survival. I just have to hold onto it.

Somewhere as a child, the cold-and-hunger dance passed into me.

Awkward. Intrusive. A routine of writing and rewriting and rewriting and wait.

I'm always thinking about the importance of story. I've heard many Native American writers say that our words are our most important possession. They define what we are.

Stories give us our sense of meaning. But what exactly is a story? How does it work?

Dan Taylor, in *The Healing Power of Stories* (Doubleday, 1996), says that "a story is the telling of the significant actions of characters over time." But where should the definition go from there?

When I was in Germany, I visited the Forum der Technik, the science museum, in Munich. On the second floor, I saw a huge DNA double helix. Somehow I thought, that's how a story works.

Our lives are made of the joining of words into stories into meaning into integral parts of our being. In the same way, maybe, that we're made of DNA, which carries the chemical traditions from generation to generation.

There also was an explanation of genetic coding on the second floor of the museum, and though it was in German, I could see two things linking. I felt, likewise, our minds hold up their hands to hook onto a story. A possibility of meaning. The mind and the story connect and coil with other stories to form the structure of thought. There is a combining of elements.

Later, I was reminded of Reginald Gibbon's comment about the chapters of the novella "Monkey Secret": "threaded with the twin strands" of Jean Pierce's culture and her love for her cousin. There are always undercurrents working in the subconscious to make connections.

When I returned from Germany, Jim Straka, biochemist and visiting professor at Macalester College, talked to me about the DNA I had seen in Germany, since the language explaining it, as I said, had been in German. As he told me about A, T, G, C, the four bases on the strands of DNA, we agreed the DNA structure could be a metaphor for story.

There was the possibility of a correspondance.

The meaning and sound of the spoken words, the hearing and interpretation of them, the telling of them again in one's own way.

The four bases holding hands. Their carefulness in which hands they hold.

The DNA making protein, which, in combination with the DNA, makes cells to make organs to make organisms. There is a circularity in the fact that DNA makes protein that is necessary to make more DNA.

As story must be heard and processed to make more story.

The drift and change.

Somehow I could make the transference.

It's always been those small connections. I was living in Oklahoma when I met Gerald Stern at a writers' conference in Tucson. He encouraged me to apply to the Iowa Writer's Workshop. I was living in the farmhouse I rented in Iowa when Alvin Greenberg called from Macalester College. Could I come up and look the school over? He'd heard my name at an Associated Writing Program's conference where he asked for names when he was thinking of changing and expanding the English department faculty.

And I was there with determination like flint that was going to spark. I came from no intellectual tradition or background. I was supposed to be quiet, invisible, to survive. But I could feel the fortifier moving. I could feel the spark of the human mind.

I could move to Minnesota and teach. I could step to one place after another in the landscape of the classroom: writing and Native American literature. I could take one trip after another in a continual migration of readings: from the Hungry Mind Bookstore in St. Paul to the Loft in Minneapolis to the University of Alabama in Tuscaloosa to the Phillips Public Library in Eau Claire, Wisconsin, to the Summer Writer's Conference at the University of Iowa in Iowa City to the just buffalo literary center in Buffalo, New York, to the Library in Olean, New York, to the Conference on Christianity and Literature at Baylor University in Waco, Texas, to Southwestern Oklahoma State University in Weatherford to the Quartz Mountain Writer's Conference in Lone Wolf, Oklahoma, to Hope College, Holland, Michigan, to a reading at the University of Alabama in Huntsville to a Writer's Conference at Concordia College in Moorhead, Minnesota, to the University of Rochester in Rochester, New York, to the University of Arizona in

Tucson to the Conference for the Short Story in Ames, Iowa, to the Arts Guild Complex in Chicago to the Matthews Opera House in Spearfish, South Dakota, to Northland College in Ashland, Wisconsin, to the Left Bank Bookstore for the Writer and Religion Conference at Washington University in St. Louis to the Modern Language Association presentation of my play "Halfact" in San Diego.

I could take research trips, driving back along the Trail of Tears from Georgia, Tennessee, Kentucky, Illinois, Missouri, Arkansas, and Oklahoma, stopping at state parks and museums along the way. In the same two-year period, I could travel to the Rosebud Reservation and drive across Montana. I could fly to the Squaw Valley Writers' Conference in California for a screenwriting workshop. I could drive to Provincetown, Massachusetts, for a month's fellowship. Another time, I could drive through New England.

I could spend two months in Australia. I could go to Japan in addition to the USIS trips. All of which I've done and written about in my poems and stories and novels and creative nonfiction.

I could be a reader of manuscripts for Fiction Collective II, the University of Oklahoma Press, and the North American Indian Prose Award for the University of Nebraska Press. I could be on the 1995 National Endowment for the Arts Panel, the Jerome Travel Grant Panel, and serve as judge for poetry competitions.

I could follow the turns of narrative truth in their pivotal and moving processes. Their several directions and points of departures and returns. I could see truth as a collaborative work, a country of imagination, a series of integral histories integrated into how one reads the narrative.

In other words, my words could be about the impossibility of arriving at one place of wholeness, but getting somewhere in the neighborhood.

I could feel the parts of myself, unthreaded even by my name, with an Indian name someone gave me which means "Happy Butterfly Woman." A name I would need in the moving and changing places I've lived my life. I was named after my Aunt Helen, my mother's sister. But I've never been called by that name, though it appears as my name on official documents. And my married name speaks of a heritage I don't have. But when I married, a long time ago, I don't remember the option of keeping my own name or returning to it once I had children.

I've turned one blank space after another forming my identity, but all those spaces, threaded one after another, coiling together like rope, is who I am.

Aunt Mil Wood in her saddle shoes and Uncle Carl Wood with
my father and mother, Lewis and Edith Hall, on the running board
of Uncle Carl's '39 Oldsmobile on my grandparent's farm,
five months before I was born. October 13, 1940

Sitting on the fortified wall. *My rock and fortress*—Psalm 31:3. August 22, 1941

My mother and me. November 24, 1941

I remember the empty bookcases beside the fireplace in our living room.
I don't remember having many books. Yet, I'm on the front steps
of my house, age 2 1/2, reading. October 17, 1943

Ready for church. April 16, 1950

My father with my brother, David, and me. September 8, 1944

My hands in the white frost of the keys. May 25, 1950

My brother and me at the Pacific. July 1950

My cousin, Susan, who is Aunt Helen's daughter, and me
on our grandparents' farm. February 4, 1951

My brother and me at Itasca. July 10, 1951

My first dance in my fairy-wand dress. May 1956

My brother, my parents, and me in front of our house
in St. Louis. May 1959

My brother, my mother, and me. May 12, 1957

A chilly afternoon at my house in St. Paul. April 18, 1996
photo by Jim Turnure

The Autobiography of My Life with Jesus

I think they brought me a picture of Jesus with the lambs, and there was a black one, and I think they pointed to it and said Jesus loved the black sheep, the lost sheep. Somehow they must have sensed I was or would be. Or the Holy Spirit told them. I have come to believe that's true. I don't remember Jesus again for a while except that He was the staff I leaned on. I couldn't see Him, but I knew He was there. Somehow He was the shepherd. The children were around Him then, and how the sheep turned into children I cannot say, but somehow the transformation happened without my notice.

Jesus is my shepherd. My staff, as I have said.

I see His footprints on the crumpled moon. Every night He steps to the earth. He goes to those dark villages in the desert and unloads their guns. He feeds rice to the camels. He calls the radio waves and broadcasts.

How long I have hoped to put my foot in Galilee.

Still I wait.

He gives me faith.

Jesus is my Earhart.

My flight jacket.

My straw fan on a summer afternoon when I was supposed to sleep. I don't know why I had to take naps. Sleep was like a herd of avocados in my hand.

Sometimes I fall on the bed in my bare feet, the straps of a pinafore or sundress over my shoulders. I feel His invisible staff. I remember when I was a girl. I lie quiet as if I were a sheep.

Sun Dance

She practiced both religions at the same
time and at random. Her soul was
healthy and at peace, she said, because
what she did not find in one faith
was there in another. — *Gabriel*
García Márquez, Of Love and
Other Demons

It was raining when I left St. Paul on Interstate 35 south for the Sun Dance on the Rosebud Reservation just west of Mission, South Dakota. It's 523 miles to the particular dance I was going to. There are others. But this one I knew through Mazakute Native American Mission in St. Paul. I went to the Sun Dance last summer, and wanted to go again to find some words to put it in perspective. To understand more than my own way. To understand why I wanted to return to a ceremony that was not in my culture.

Two hours later, at Interstate 90 in southern Minnesota, I turned west. Another four hours, and I stopped at the lookout above the Missouri River nearly halfway across South Dakota. There isn't much between the low sky and the prairie, except the Missouri River which cuts into the land. The river is green in its valley. Like one of those nineteenth-century landscapes. If you don't look at the bridge. And the traffic.

I read a plaque.

> *Lewis & Clark / 1804 / ate plums & acorns from the burr oaks / killed*
> *a buffalo & magpie / dried equipment / repacked boats / camped again*
> 1806 *on the return trip.*

I felt the raised letters on the plaque with my hand as if they were the low hills. I ran my finger between them as if my finger were the river. I thought of the site of the Mandan village farther north on the

Missouri, where another plaque says the whole tribe was wiped out by smallpox.

A few hours later, I exited Interstate 90 at Murdo. I took Highway 83 south for the last sixty-three miles of the trip. At the junction of Highway 18, I turned west a short distance, then south again at a sign that says *Mission*. Later I turned onto Highway 1, with the *1* on an arrowhead. Somewhere, after one turn or another, the road to Mission goes east and the open land of the Rosebud Reservation is west. The highway descended into a sharp valley, curved around a gas station and convenience store, and a few buildings of Sinte Gleska College, then climbed the hill. No name of the town. No names on streets. Nothing to let you know where you are. At the top of the hill, I turned south again at a sign marked *St. Francis*. Somehow the roads shift and boundaries are not remembered once you passed.

My ears popped and the land seemed high under the sky. I saw a butte to the west and the gray trail of the highway up and down across the land to the south. And it rained. I watched the cattle grazing through the nodding wipers. I passed the Rosebud Timber Reserve, a few clumps of pastel reservation houses, some with satellite dishes, and a trail of smoke from the garbage burn.

In St. Francis, I found the water tower road and turned west on BIA 105. It was about seven miles to the ridge where the Sun Dance is held. Soon I saw the large camp of tents and teepees. I left the road and drove through the rutted field toward the north section where I found people I knew from St. Paul.

The field is on a ridge high above a valley filled with pines. It's pasture except for the third week in July when it's used for the Sun Dance. I passed the vans and trucks and cars, the teepees and tents, the Coleman stoves and campfires. Children ran everywhere and groups of people sat by their tents. It stopped raining and the smell of cedar and sage and cooking fires filled the air.

In the center of the camp is the Sun Dance arena, which looked like an old brush-arbor church-camp meeting in Oklahoma. But this was the Sun Dance and I was going to see it on its own terms.

In the middle of the Sun Dance arena is the cottonwood tree that had been cut and carried into the circle and placed upright again. The cottonwood because it holds water. Its branches were tied up with ropes, and prayer ties or tobacco ties hung from the tree. Black for West. Red for North. Yellow for East. White for South. Green for Earth. Blue for Sky.

It was evening and everyone was resting. After the nine-hour trip from St. Paul by myself, I pulled a borrowed tent from my car and unfolded it. Others helped me set it up.

In the dark, I moved my sleeping bag several places on the hard, uneven ground inside the tent.

I slept, and at 4:30 I heard the wake-up song on the loud speaker. There was no reason to get up. I was an observer. I knew the sun dancers were on their way to the sweat lodges for purification. When I heard the drums, I knew they began in the first light, in their long skirts and bare chests, moving inside the circle of the arena around the cottonwood, singing the Sun Dance songs and blowing their eagle-bone whistles. The women danced in a larger circle around the men.

Soon I got up and walked to the brush arbor, which surrounded both circles of dancers and the tree.

Others watched as the piercing began. A man who had danced and prayed and was in the right frame of mind lay on the buffalo robe by the tree in the center of the circle. Two elk bone skewers were pushed under the skin on his chest. He stood connected to the tree with two small ropes and joined his group of supporters in the circle that surrounded the tree for however many rounds he chose. Then he pulled back on the ropes until the skewers broke free and he was released.

Men are not suspended from a pole, nor do they stare at the sun until they're blind. The Sun Dance is a commitment, more a way of life than a religion. It's keeping a promise. Doing what you say you're going to do. It's a prayer service to the Great Spirit. An intercession for relatives in need. It's humility and respect and supplication. It's a strengthening ceremony. A thanksgiving.

There were testimonies between rounds. And the humor of the announcer mixed with the endurance, the suffering, the seriousness. Over and over, the announcer said to pray for the dancers who were having a difficult time in their fight against heat, thirst, hunger, and tiredness.

There was an assortment of people from several states at the Sun Dance. The Indians are mainly Lakota and Dakota. They open their ceremony to others. There were many white people. Some come from Europe. One family was from Australia. I don't know numbers. Maybe there were four hundred. Probably more. Cars came and went each day.

It was an old ceremony of death and resurrection. A connection to the tree. A release.

The Sun Dance continued all day until about 6:00. Then the dancers sat once more in the sweat lodge and returned to their tents or teepees. They cannot eat or drink water.

There are those who are pierced. There are those who just dance. There are those who watch. I stood in the brush arbor that circled the dance arena. For the second year, I forgot a lawn chair. I watched. Prayed. Thought of my own needs and others. Danced in place. Raised my hands to the tree like the dancers and the other watchers. Sometimes I walked back to the tent. I made tobacco prayer ties that someone would hang on the tree. I was not part of the Sun Dance and could not enter the arena.

There are many rules.

For lunch I ate peanut butter on crackers, remembering somehow the burr oak acorns and magpies from the Missouri River plaque. I drank warm water out of a plastic bottle. You carry your water and food in with you. Whatever you need. I was reminded of church camp in Oklahoma when I had to put on my socks over dirty feet and felt the dust between my toes. There's an outhouse but no bath or shower. You camp in an open field under the sun on a ridge above the valleys of dark pines maybe 150 or 200 miles southeast of the Black Hills. By midafternoon the heat was unbearable inside the tent. The only shade was in the arbor where sometimes a warm breeze moved the prayer ties on the tree.

That night I drove into Mission to hear an Indian leader. He began with a story about a minister who led his congregation in a hymn from the church, only he was walking backward as he led them, and at the edge of the churchyard he fell into a newly dug grave and couldn't get out, his head appearing and disappearing as he jumped. Finally they pulled him out, and he had that white soil even in his eyebrows. The Indian leader used the laughter to enter the hardship of living, the meanness of reservation border towns. When you pray for us, he said, pray for alcoholism, AIDS, drugs, diabetes, joblessness, poverty.

I started back to the Sun Dance ground around 9:30. The sun had gone down and the sky was like a piece of blue tissue paper. Some thought or memory was wrapped in it. The land was dark and wavy beneath the sky. There was one star up there, and the telephone poles were crosses on the hills.

I thought it was about thirty miles back from Mission. I knew it was a long way and I felt unsure. It was hard to see the road in the dark. There was just the prairie and the sky and the centerline on the road and watching the shoulders for deer.

Sometimes, far off in the distance, I saw a few lights on the horizon. I thought it must be St. Francis, but the lights didn't seem in the right direction. The road wasn't headed toward them. I passed a lone building with a yard light. A schoolbus parked in a yard. And where were the stars? The sky in the west still had not turned out its light. Maybe it was too early for them.

Yes, the few lights I saw were St. Francis. The highway finally curved toward them. On the water tower road, right after the post office, I turned west. I wondered if I could see the camp off BIA 501 in the dark. I wondered if I would know when seven miles went by. There was a car behind me and I didn't want to go too slow. But soon I saw car lights coming through a field. I knew the turnoff was just ahead. I signaled, and the car behind me also turned, its headlights on bright.

As I looked from my tent that night, I saw the stars. A sky full of them. I went to sleep on the lumpy ground.

At 4:30 this morning, I got up. I wasn't comfortable. I wanted to leave. I was into something I didn't belong in. A Sun Dance in the Lakota-Dakota tradition. I was in a magnetic field and I felt repelled. But I have felt outside of every tradition I've been in. The Methodist church as a child because I couldn't figure out all the trouble of going to church. What did they preach other than the brotherhood of man and a sense of community? I needed more than that.

I needed salvation to help me out of the hurt and isolation and darkness I felt. The hardship of my own life. The years I'd worked. The invisibility I felt. The reservation border town that writing seemed to be. The weight of years pulling my children through the pitfalls. My daughter in college and law school calling saying she didn't know if she could do it, just think of the student loans she'll be buried under for years.

I had also attended the Presbyterian church through the years, which seemed to me like the Methodist. And later, the fundamentalist church I went to was opposed to the arts and a life of the imagination. Sometimes I attended the Episcopal church.

There was no belonging here either. I was from not the north but a shadow of a place where I used to live, but I wasn't from there either. I was born long ago, to parents of different heritages. I'd lived several places and none of them is where I'm from.

I felt marginalization from both my white and Indian heritages. I was neither of both. Both of neither. My great-grandfather was a full-blood Cherokee born near Sallisaw in Indian Territory in 1843. His parents got there somehow. The only way was the Trail of Tears from the southeast. My mother's people of European descent farmed in Kansas.

Because I didn't have a road, because I was in the process of the journey, I still didn't know why I was between two different cultures. I still had to jump-start an image of my broken self.

The Bible is full of journeys. It's why I think it is home.

That second morning at the Sun Dance, I watched the men lie on the buffalo robe. I watched as the holy men pushed the skewers under their skin. That's where it suddenly connected for me.

My son, when he was 17, had open lung surgery. He had holes in his lungs and they had to be stapled. When his lung first collapsed, the doctor pushed a tube into his chest. I was sitting outside the curtain. The opening for the tube was the size of a yellow jacket stinging with a stinging he couldn't push away.

I was not an outsider to this. I am the mother who listened to him suffer. I smoked and drank when he was conceived, and those habits interfered with his chances for development. I think so anyway. I've had a dream of snow in the yard. He was looking from the window. I tossed the snow at the window calling him until he disappeared.

He was born blue and mottled. Wrapped in the tissue paper of the evening sky. There was also a second surgery. His kidney, that time. He was pierced in the side like Christ, and not all the pages of the Bible can change it.

I wished I could go back and conceive him again. I wished I could put on his overalls and pull a shirt over his chest again. He survived. He went through officer training at Quantico and spent four years in the Marines. He went back to school and now teaches.

That morning in the open field on the Rosebud Reservation in South Dakota, during one of the rest periods between the rounds of dancing, an elder spoke over the loudspeaker. He said the Sun Dance is a form of Christ going to the cross. For me, it was finished on the cross. But the ceremony of linkage to suffering and release is still here, in this manger of sorts, this place where cattle usually graze. This place where boats unload and repack to start back on the river.

In the afternoon, I drove with two friends to the White River, nearly to Murdo. I heard the birds and insects in the grasses from the window of the car as I passed, like Oklahoma and the open places I've traveled. We picked some sage in a field along the road, leaving an offering of tobacco.

We had lunch at the Cook Shack in Mission and returned to the Sun Dance grounds for another hot afternoon. That evening as the dance finished, the announcer said there was a severe storm warning. We could see the clouds to the west because you can see far across the prairie from the ridge where we camped. Less than an hour later, we were in our tents trying to hold them down in the wind.

That evening I rode out the storm in the borrowed tent, the sides puffing as if it were a large bird trying to take flight. I heard the snap and hum of the lightning. I could even smell it.

Afterwards, while it was still light, I heard someone say, *look at the rainbows*. When I looked from the tent, I saw the two rainbows over the camp grounds. I stood in the slight rain that was still falling and the wind still whipping the tents and felt the oneness with the sky and earth. I felt survival. I felt promise. I felt what I hadn't known I'd been looking for. Significance.

Later in the night, I heard the eerie noise of coyotes, the hecklers, laughing at what I had found. But I stuck with it.

I wanted a journey of meaning in ordinary life. I'd always liked the plain land under the sky. The routine of housework and grading papers and writing and teaching and traveling, transformed by the act of its own ordinariness. Just as Jesus walking through the wheat field, these moments became more than themselves.

My mother used to talk about the Maypole dance she experienced as a girl. The ceremony of the tree goes back in history. The cross of Christ. The cottonwood tree of the Sun Dance. It is a connection to the past.

> *. . . I hung*
> *on the windy tree . . .*
> *gashed with a blade*
> *bloodied for Odinn*
>   *myself an offering to myself*
> *knotted to that tree*
> *no man knows*
>   *wither the roots of it run.*
> — Dr. Brian Branston, The Last Gods of England

The Sun Dance is also a connection to the Plains Indian culture I had read about in school, which is different from the woodland Cherokee heritage my father had left. It always left me with a sense of confusion as to what an *Indian* was.

I know now I was looking for meaning in the heat and community and sometimes the boredom as a Sun Dance observer.

I knew I already had it. When my son's chest was opened during surgery, when I had come apart, when I needed the construct of strength and meaning and hope, it was Christ. I've always gone to church through the years. I was saved and filled with the Holy Spirit. I spoke in tongues.

I believe in ceremony. There were many ceremonies at the Sun Dance, which is itself a ceremony.

The next morning, the clouds were low when I dismantled my tent and left. It felt as if the day would be cool, but I knew how soon the heat comes.

I watched the road ahead of me as I drove back toward Interstate 90 to the north. I watched the road's reflection on the hood of my car. I had made an expedition to a place I was not from. The low, rolling hills of South Dakota under the sky that lidded them. I felt the air in the window. My hand on the wheel.

I turned east onto Interstate 90 toward Minnesota. The cars and trucks moving along the highway were unaware of the Sun Dance just a few miles over the hills. And the Sun Dancers, when they came in their vans with their teepee lodgepoles tied on top and turned onto the Interstate, would pass along the road with the other traffic. They would carry with them their *significance*, which is a blanket over the pitfalls of the earth. Well, we do fall into them sometimes, but get lifted out.

It's why I wanted to write — to touch words — because the touch of words was alive.

The House of Him Who Hath
His Shoe Loosed

—Deuteronomy 25:10

It was a law that if a brother dies and has no child, the wife could not marry outside the family, but her husband's brother would take her for a wife and the first-born would be named for the dead brother. If the man didn't want his brother's wife, she could untie his shoe in front of the elders at the gate of the city.

What did it mean to walk without a shoe? Or to walk with one shoe loosed? Could the man lean down and tie it up again? Did he have to walk in the desert without a shoe? Could he run if someone chased him?

It's unexplained, as are those other laws.

An excerpt that was told. The whole left to be somehow understood. Or filled in later. Or reverberating in another place.

Thou shalt not plow with an ox and an ass.

Thou shalt not wear wool and linen together.

The unlaced shoe was a sign that his brother would go without a name in Israel. He had not done what he should have done. Like the rest of the human race.

One-shoed. Off-balanced. Wishing the laces were tied.

Photography

Photographs furnish evidence.

*To write about photography is to
appropriate the photographs.*
—*Susan Sontag,* On Photography

1.

These little truth serums.
These little preachers that do not lie.
They line up in the album like a firing squad.
They are a slow disease of successive years that change appearance.

2.

The evidence I have of my mother's life is the photograph albums
I inherited—took rather—from her closet shelf. Most of the photographs are family gatherings. Cousins and aunts and uncles at July
Fourth picnics. My brother and I holding our Easter baskets.

Then the grandparents disappear. My father. One by one, others are
not there. Slowly, the next generation appears.

3.

My mother's stage was her photography. Her characters were photographed as if clothes hanging in a closet, as if the thirty-nine Dakotas
hanged after the 1864 uprising in Mankato, Minnesota.

4.

We were her marionettes.
She moved us with the strings of the camera.
Her finger opened the lens like an oven door.

5.

The four directions for my mother were cooking, cleaning the house,
washing and ironing, and smoking her cigarette in the overstuffed chair

by the front door. Photography was the center pole. That fifth direction from which the others radiated.

6.
Looking through her photo albums, I knew my mother had dreams she never realized.

Her camera was her war against the nondocumentation from which she came. Or maybe an itinerant photographer came by the farm like a god clothed in his box that replicated her. And she heard him say, Be fruitful, and multiply, fill the earth; have dominion. (Genesis 1:28.)

Somehow the photographs took away her fig leaf and clothed her with animal skins.

7.
Her philosophy of photography: Line them up and shoot.

8.
I know my birth was hard on her because of the absence of photos. I was dark and my darkness hid in the bassinet or inside the white sunbonnet. Later I showed up, when she had adjusted, and there were a lot of pictures then.

9.
She was the god of marionettes.

Her principles were placement, light, standing still, and silence.

Her photographs still hold me with their strings.

10.
I don't own a camera.

11.
I return to the photographs like a piano practice piece. I look at the photo of me wearing a corsage, my hair curled, my hands in the white frost of the keys.

Her world fell on me like snow.

I could not walk in it.

My identity was a hand pushing me back. My identity was a pose. A representation of what I was.

A fig leaf, an animal skin. The shedding of blood, mainly hers, to clothe me.

My father shed blood too, in the stockyards where he worked. The cattle were driven up a ramp into the slaughter room. Their throats were slit, they were pulled upside-down over a trough where their blood drained. They were cut into sections. Their parts carted down the hall.

In the same way, I entered her album and came out dressed.

12.

I think of the extremes of heat and cold in the kitchen. The oven, the refrigerator. A white trail of piano keys that got pushed down.

13.

The photographs grew fewer and fewer each year as she grew older and unhappier and heavier. As her life grew smaller, mine enlarged, my tulle dress for a dance hanging in the album as if a fairy wand.

14.

Maybe my mother's photography *iconizes* the photographs, but her stillnesses of what moved keep us slow dancing in her albums. In the act of her successive placements, she swallowed the past. If the photos hang in her albums like bodies from a gallows, it's because the past is death to whatever stood there. Yet she reconstructed the family through her photos.

They are magic.

They are coup sticks.

They are the soldiers who shoot and the ones who die.

The Bible and Black Elk Speaks

I think *Black Elk Speaks* is the Native American version of the Bible. Especially the book of Revelation. In fact, I think it's America's version. Black Elk belongs to our continent. He was born in 1863. His vision was just over a hundred years ago. John Neihardt's transcription of Black Elk's words was first published by William Morrow in 1932. Recent history, it seems to me.

Black Elk's narrative happened during the close of the Plains Indian history. In the years that led to the 1890 Battle of Wounded Knee in South Dakota, when the cavalry opened fire on the Ghost Dancers, who were trying to make their world come back.

Among Native people there had been visions of the spirit world and prophecies of a coming doom. One of those seers was Black Elk. Like the book of Revelation's John on Patmos, Black Elk left the earth in a vision. He says, "While I was there I saw more than I can tell and I understood more than I saw; for I was seeing in a sacred manner the shapes of all things in the spirit" (John Neihardt, *Black Elk Speaks* [Lincoln: University of Nebraska Press, 1988], 43).

Black Elk's life, as well as his vision, centered on the change in the way of life that was coming for the Indian. Cataclysmic events. During the massacre at Wounded Knee, an Indian people and their way of living passed into the other world. Though the Indian people also survived and their culture is still vital, they suffered an apocalypse. Much of what they had known was gone.

In Black Elk's vision, the spirit world was revealing the end of one focus and the beginning of another. In describing one part of his vision, Black Elk said

I saw . . . a sacred man who was painted red all over his body, and he held a spear as he walked into the center of the people and there he lay down and rolled. And when he got up, it was a fat bison standing there, and where the bison stood a sacred herb sprang up right where the tree had been in the center of the nation's hoop. . . . I know now what this meant, that the bison were the gift of a good spirit and were our strength, but we should lose them, and from the same good spirit we must find another strength. (38–39)

As I am a Christian, this man painted red makes me think of John's vision of Christ:

And he was clothed with a vesture dipped in blood; and his name is called The Word of God. (Revelation 19:13)

Thou art worthy to take the scroll and to open its seal; for thou wast slain, and hast redeemed us to God by thy blood. (Revelation 5:9)

Black Elk was a holy man of the Oglala Sioux. Dakota, they're called now. No, Lakota. Between Manderson and Pine Ridge. Where John Neihardt, a white, Poet Laureate of Nebraska, went in 1930 to hear Black Elk:

It was when I was five years old that my Grandfather made me a bow and some arrows. The grass was young and I was on horseback. A thunder storm was coming from where the sun goes down, and just as I was riding into the woods along a creek, there was a kingbird sitting on a limb. This was not a dream, it happened. And I was going to shoot at the kingbird with the bow my Grandfather made, when the bird spoke and said: "the clouds all over are one-sided." Perhaps it meant that all the clouds were looking at me. And then it said: "Listen. A voice is calling you!" Then I looked up at the clouds, and two men were coming there, head-first like arrows slanting down; and as they came, they sang a sacred song and the thunder was like drumming. I will sing it for you. The song and the drumming were like this: "Behold a sacred voice is calling you; all over the sky a sacred voice is calling."

I sat there gazing at them, and they were coming from the place where the giant lives (north). But when they were close to me, they wheeled about toward where the sun goes down, and suddenly they were geese. Then they were gone, and the rain came with a big wind and a roaring. (18–19)

As I said, John Neihardt was a white man, and I know some Native Americans say that in changing Black Elk's words from oral to written form, Neihardt didn't "get it right." In fact, when Black Elk told his story to Neihardt, it was interpreted through Black Elk's son, Ben, and sometimes supplemented by some of Black Elk's friends, then transcribed by Enid, Neihardt's daughter, whom Neihardt called "a skilled stenographer." Then Neihardt retold it all in his own words, of course, and maybe the text shifted somewhat and Black Elk didn't mean what *Black Elk Speaks* says he meant. But that isn't known for sure. Then to further complicate matters, I'm interpreting the book to mean what I think it means from my own heritage — part evangelical Christian and white, part Cherokee, which is a different culture from Lakota, and a different denomination from Black Elk's Catholicism. In December 1904, he had been baptised into the Catholic faith as Nick Black Elk. So how can anyone know anything? Which is what modern theory asks. But that's what storying is. You say your voice from others, and some of your voice comes off. That's the way the Bible, the holy book of the white man, or some of the white men, is written. The four gospels tell the story of Jesus, each in their own voice, the way creation is told and retold or added to, in Genesis 1:1–2:3 and again in Genesis 2:4–25. It's the same listening to all the Old Testament voices tell their side of the story. I prefer the *accumulation* style, anyway, to the self-referential Paul.

Which gets to my point:

I cannot read *Black Elk Speaks* without thinking about the Bible, especially the book of Revelation.

Now this is John on Patmos:

After this I looked and, behold, a door was opened in heaven; and the first voice that I heard was, as it were, of a trumpet talking with me; which said, Come up here, and I will show thee things which must be hereafter. And immediately I was in the Spirit, and behold, a throne was set in heaven, and one sat on the throne. (Revelation 4:1–2)

And this is Black Elk in the chapter "The Great Vision":

there were two men coming from the clouds, head-first like arrows slanting down, and I knew they were the same that I had seen before. . . . They came clear down to the ground this time and stood a little way off and looked at me and said: "Hurry! Come! Your Grandfathers are calling you!" . . .

Then there was nothing but air and the swiftness of the little cloud that bore me . . . where white clouds were piled like mountains . . . and the thunder beings lived and leaped and flashed. (22)

The two men in Black Elk's vision are alone with Black Elk in the middle of a great white plain with snowy hills. Black Elk sees a horse and then there are twelve horses in each of the four directions, some wearing elk-teeth necklaces, some with manes that lived and grew like trees and grasses. And then there are dancing horses without number. They change into animals and birds. Then the clouds around Black Elk change into a teepee, and a rainbow is the open door of it; and through the door are six old men, which are the powers of the world. One of the Grandfathers speaks and tells Black Elk he will be a healer of his people. Then he says

"Behold the earth!" So I looked down and saw it lying yonder like a hoop of peoples, and in the center bloomed the holy stick that was a tree. (29)

And John the Evangelist:

And he showed me a pure river of water of life, clear as crystal, proceeding out of the throne of God and of the Lamb. In the midst of the street of it, and on either side of the river, was there the tree of life, which bore twelve kinds of fruits, and yielded her fruit every month; and the leaves of the tree were for the healing of nations. (Revelation 22:1–2)

There are further complications to my "Christian" interpretation of *Black Elk Speaks*. And that is, which version or brand of Christianity among the many am I talking about? I define Christianity as salvation through faith in the blood of Christ. A Christian is not necessarily one who belongs to a certain denomination, nor one who lives by doctrine or tries to do good works, but one who recognizes that Christ's death on the cross is the basis for God's acceptance.

Jesus said, I am the way, the truth and the life; no man cometh unto the Father, but by me. (John 14:6)

In other words, the Great Spirit has a world I'm invited to — but I cannot enter except on His terms.

I sometimes think of Indian tradition as the Old Testament, so to speak. The way Christ is confounding to the Jews. At least I read that into it. And that's what storying is. A jump. An attempt to reach another realm. A push through to what I'm not sure of. But needs to be jumped through to. Or jumped at, I think. Yes, the bison is the ark of the covenant for the Indian. And some Indians have rejected Black Elk's sacred red man just as Jews rejected Christ.

Now this is something that's going to make some people mad. But America is about democracy. There's freedom of speech and religion. I can be a Christian. I can say I think John and Black Elk both saw Christ in their own way. I can talk about my faith. I can talk about what I think. Even when it disagrees with some fundamental things others believe.

Now listen to this:

In the . . . Sierras . . . before you come to the big water, there was a sacred man among the Paiutes who had talked to the Great Spirit in a vision, and the Great Spirit had told him how to . . . make the Wasichus (white man) disappear and bring back the bison and the people who were dead and how there would be a new earth. . . . The people sent three men, Good Thunder, Brave Bear, and Yellow Breast to see this sacred man. . . .

[When they came back to] White Clay Creek, not far from Pine Ridge, . . . they said they traveled until they came to a place called Mason Valley, Nevada, and there they saw the Wanekia, who was the son of the Great Spirit, and they talked to him. Wasichus called him Jack Wilson, but his name was Wovoka. He told them that there was another world coming, just like a cloud. It would come in a whirlwind out of the west and would crush everything in the world, which was old and dying. . . .

This sacred man gave some sacred red paint and two eagle feathers to Good Thunder. The people must put this on their faces and they must dance a ghost dance that the sacred man taught to Good Thunder, Yellow Breast, and Brave Bear. If they danced, they could get on this other world when it came, and the Wasichus would not be able to get on, and so they would disappear. . . .

I heard the gossip that was everywhere now, and people said it was really the son of the Great Spirit who was out there; that when he came to the Wasichus a long time ago, they had killed him; but he was coming to the Indians this time and there would not be any Wasichus in the new world that would come like a cloud in a whirlwind and crush out the old earth that was dying. (232–235)

This is cross-referenced in a speech by Kicking Bear near Pine Ridge in 1890 in the book *Indian Oratory,* compiled by W. C. Vanderwerth and published by the University of Oklahoma Press in 1989. The years when the Indians' years closed. The Battle of Wounded Knee when soldiers killed the Indians who Ghost Danced. But if you look at it from apocolytic–rapture-believing–Christian eyes, maybe the bison and ancestors were there to meet them at the door of death. Who knows.

Under the South Dakota sky.

I never had trouble believing that other world was there. I always thought there was something going on behind what I could see. I always needed to think so anyway. I got it from the Bible and from books like *Black Elk Speaks.* From a feeling of incompleteness without it. From a hollowness in my own heart. From trips to my father's Cherokee people. Which my white mother hated. Because of their superstition, which seems to me now the hard fact that other things *happen*. We have connection to earth and sky and ancestors. But my father's people weren't traditional. The Keetowah society. All that. But Christian. Many Cherokees are Baptists. Other denominations also. Since living here in the Plains area, I'm more aware of the *difference* of the Cherokees from other Indians. In fact, the vast differences between all Indian peoples is a preliminary to understanding.

But there were connectives between both heritages of my family. Between Sunday School and *story*. In each creation story, Genesis and Cherokee —

> Let the waters under the heaven be gathered together into one place, and let the dry land appear. (Genesis 1:9)

> A piece of mud was placed on the water which grew into land. (from a Cherokee creation story)

In other words, there was nothing and then there was something. There also are similar passages about the sky in the midst of water:

> Let there be a firmament in the midst of the waters, and let it divide the waters from the waters. (Genesis 1:6)

> And God called the firmament Heaven. (Genesis 1:8)

> Now there was a wooden cup in his hand and it was full of water and in the water was the sky. (*Black Elk*, 26)

I have always wondered how it was possible to combine both religions. The down-home Bible-belt Christianity. The Indian no-boundaried magical. But I had to do it. To make a dry ground in the midst of the uncertainty of my own life and my belief system or spirituality.

It still isn't easy. Part of the liturgy at Mazakute Church in St. Paul says, "We pray that all members of Creation will be respected as relatives to all-that-is." So how does the Christian who also has native blood hear the apostle Paul? According to him, in his Letter to the Romans, honoring animals may mean worshiping the creation more than the Creator. How can such opposite thoughts be reconciled?

But some of the things Black Elk says sounds like the Bible:

Here we shall raise our children and be as little chickens under the mother sheo's wing. (34)

In the shadow of thy wings will I make my refuge. (Psalms 57:1)

That was David speaking. God also uses similar imagery:

how often I have gathered my children together, even as a hen gathereth her chickens under her wings. (Matthew 23:37)

Black Elk and the Bible both warn against following personal visions:

Each one seemed to have his own little vision that he followed and his own rules; and all over the universe I could hear the winds at war like wild beasts fighting. (37)

In those days, there was no king in Israel, but every man did that which was right in his own eyes. (Judges 17:6)

And that there's more important stuff than the body:

It does not matter where his body lies, for it is grass; but where his spirit is, it will be good to be. (145)

As for a man, his days are like the grass. (Psalms 103:15)

All flesh is grass. (Isaiah 40:6)

And that we are not limited to our circumstances:

We were fighting and retreating, and all at once I saw Red Willow on foot running. He called to me: "Cousin, my horse is killed!" So I caught up a soldier's horse that was dragging a rope and brought it to Red Willow while the soldiers were shooting fast at me. Just then, for a little while, I was a *wanekia* myself. (269)

I can do all things through Christ who strengtheneth me. (Philippians 4:13)

Yet there's humility at the same time:

I got off my horse and rubbed earth on myself, to show the Powers that I was nothing without their help. (265)

And I, brethren, when I came to you, came not with excellency of speech or of wisdom, declaring unto you the testimony of God. And I was with you in weakness, and in fear, and in much trembling. And my speech and my preaching were not with enticing words of man's wisdom, but in demonstration of the Spirit and of power; That your faith should not stand in the wisdom of men, but in the power of God. (I Corinthians 2:1, 3–5)

And that there are many voices in the world, and it's difficult to be faithful:

It is hard to follow one great vision in this world of darkness and of many changing shadows. (250)

He also that receiveth seed among the thorns is he that heareth the word, and the care of this world . . . chokes the word and he becomes unfaithful. (Matthew 13:22)

When I read, "his voice was not loud, but it went all over the universe and filled it," (*Black Elk Speaks*, 41) I think of the still, small voice of God (I Kings 19:12) and the voice that had the sound of many waters (Revelation 1:15). In Black Elk's "You have noticed that everything an Indian does is in a circle" speech from the chapter "The First Cure," I hear Ecclesiastes.

I also think of the similarity between the concept of faith and works:

a man who has a vision is not able to use the power of it until after he has performed the vision on earth for the people to see. (204)

Not every one that saith unto me, Lord, Lord, shall enter into the kingdom of heaven, but he that doeth the will of my Father, who is in heaven. (Matthew 7:21)

What doth it profit, my brethren, though a man say he hath faith, and have not works? Can faith save him? (James 2:14)

Now this is in the same Bible that says, *By grace are ye saved through faith; and that not of yourselves, it is the gift of God — Not of works, lest any man should boast.* — Ephesians 2:8

I like the contradictions in the Bible, and the many voices telling—the unsureness as to actuality—the relative, changing, turned-back-upon itself. That's what storytelling is. In my understanding, anyway. I also like the uncertainty I feel in Black Elk. The humanity. Black Elk also agrees with the Apostle Paul in this sense of "wretched man that I am" (Romans 7:24):

> But now that I can see it all as from a lonely hilltop, I know it was the story of a mighty vision given to a man too weak to use it; of a holy tree that should have flourished in a people's heart with flowers and singing birds, and now is withered; and of a people's dream that died in bloody snow. (1–2)

Black Elk said he had a vision given to a man who didn't understand. He regretted he saw something more than he could comprehend. But that's vision, you see. To see somewhere out of this world. Part of it moving. A changing pattern that leaves you with the feeling of defeat and inadequacy because you just can't pick up and go with it, or when you speak you're dumbfounded with all the incongruent things going on. And who would believe?

This is John on Patmos:

> And I took the little scroll out of the angel's hand and ate it up; and it was in my mouth sweet as honey, and as soon as I had eaten it my belly was bitter. (Revelation 10:10)

When Christ was on the cross, didn't He say *why have you forsaken me*? Didn't even He need to be assured now and then of who He was and what He was about? And in Luke 3:22, for instance, when "a voice came down from heaven and said, Thou art my beloved son; in thee I am well pleased" and also on the Mount of Transfiguration in the seventeenth chapter of Matthew. It seems to me, anyway, that God is assuring Jesus as much as He is us.

I believe that Jesus loved Black Elk's people so much He came to them before their apocalypse. I think He's done the same for me because I also need that same assurance. Something from part of my heritage was lost. There are many voices around me. Many things pulling at my life. I'm often uncertain. I feel the changing shapes. The brokenness:

> And I saw that the sacred hoop of my people was one of many hoops that made one circle, wide as daylight and as starlight, and in the center grew one mighty flowering tree to shelter all the children of one mother and one father. And I saw that it was holy. (43)

> In my father's house are many mansions. (John 14:2)

It's dis-arming and de-centering to know our way is only one of many. But that's what we need to see to be opened from the confinement of our hoop. It's what I think of anyway when I see the bread broken during communion. It was Christ Himself who was first broken.

It's not denomination, or group, but Christ as spirit, as story, as the living being of the Word. Sometimes, blasted by the prayer and heat in the sweat-lodge ceremony, I feel the weighty, humbling matters we face as we live.

> [The two men coming head-first like arrows flying] gave a herb to me and said: "With this on earth you shall undertake anything and do it." It was the day-break-star herb, the herb of understanding, and they told me to drop it on the earth. I saw it falling far, and when it struck the earth it rooted and grew and flowered, four blossoms on one stem, a blue, a white, a scarlet, and a yellow; and the rays from these streamed upward to the heavens so that all creatures saw it and in no place was there darkness. (43)

> Then the daybreak star was rising, and a Voice said: "It shall be a relative to them; and who shall see it, shall see much more, for thence comes wisdom; and those who do not see it shall be in dark." (35)

I think Christ is that star. I think, *It is he who sitteth upon the circle of the earth.* —Isaiah 40:22.

There shall come a star out of Jacob. (Numbers 24:17)

We have also a more sure word of prophecy, unto which ye do well that ye take heed, as unto a light that shineth in a dark place, until the day dawn, and the day star arise in your hearts. (2 Peter 1:19)

I am the bright and morning star. (Revelation 22:16)

There's also the importance of relationships in the sweat lodge, as well as the other aspects of Native American life.

This ceremony . . . had great meaning, because it made a picture of the relation between the people and the bison, and the power was in the meaning. (206)

It is from understanding that power comes; and the power in the ceremony was in understanding what it meant; for nothing can live well except in a manner that is suited to the way the sacred power of the world lives and moves. (208)

It's the multiplicity I find in meaning. The truths within Truth I can live by.

nahna adulvdi gesvi
(of that wanting which is)

We told the Indians we knew things by
written documents. The savages asked, "before
you came to the lands where we live, did you
know we were here?" *We were obliged to*
say, "no." "Then you don't know all things
through books." — *Louis Hennepin,* 1684

1.

Upstairs in the New York City Library, when I was there, there was
a line of old photos on the wall:

> A Blackfoot warrior wearing a robe
> on which was written
> *a history of his wars*
> *buffalo hunts*
> *& showing the number of scalps*
> *he has taken from his enemies*

> Tee Yee Nen Ho Ga Row, A Mahican who
> spread Christianity

> Chotan Wah Ko Wah Ma Nee, Sioux
> (the Hawk that Chases Walking)

Now there was the space between words:
Hawk was a boy and *Walking* a man (to emulate).
Or *Walking* was a girl (to love).
Another possibility was the hawk was a hawk and chased anyone
who walked.
Or perhaps the pursuit in air was slow (to glide).
Or the hawk walks instead of flying because of a wound in its wing.
Or *Hawk that Chases Walking* was a vision

at which distance from what was
left room for the self-construct of understanding,
the incision of *nahna adulvdi gesvi*
(of that wanting which is)
into the New York City Library:

the longing for possibilities of interpretation
the multiplicity needed for the understanding of meaning
the tolerance
the relativity that takes a stand
against one dominant viewpoint which leaves others out.

2.

The Ute Creation Story
Told by Ralph Cloud

it was long ago, long time ago;
the one who did it, created everything, was Sinawav;
he lived with his younger brother Coyote,
they were roaming the earth together;
only the two of them were roaming around then;
they were roaming the earth
when no one else was (alive) yet on this earth;
there was nobody (there), only the two of them;

so then he said, Sinawav did,
to his younger brother Coyote: "go cut some brush,
all kinds of brush that grows on this earth,
cut it all into real small pieces
exactly like that; not other kinds,
just from all the brush (growing) on this earth;
then pack them into this bag here";

so Coyote did as he was told,
he kept walking around doing it,
he kept walking all over; through the hills,
wherever it be,
he kept gathering all the white-blossom bushes

and the like;
Sinawav had never told him:
"Do it exactly like that"; he didn't tell him,
he had never told him (how to do it exactly);

so finally Coyote filled up his bag;
then Sinawav told him, afterwards,
when he had filled up the bag:
"Now, my little brother, go on that-a-way,
whichever direction it be, over the open country,
and keep dumping (the sticks) all over there,"
he told him, "Those sticks that you've gathered,
dump them over there," he told him;
so when Coyote went ahead, he (began wondering):
"Where is it?" he thought, Coyote did,
"What is this (that I'm carrying)?
What is it all about?
he kept thinking; perhaps I should open it
and take a look?" he thought;

so when he had gotten further away,
when Sinawav could not see him any more, he opened
it . . . he did, out they rushed,
they were people! people, all kinds of people,
whooping and hollering together, speaking . . .
speakers of many different tongues,
they whooped and hollered;
very many of them escaped,
he caught only very few of them there
and locked them back inside the bag;
but the great majority managed to escape;

now the remaining ones, later on . . .
after the others had all escaped,
that big crowd of peoples,
then he dumped them out, the few remaining ones . . .
and then he want back home;

now Sinawav knew him, the way
he had acted; so he said: "You did it, didn't you?"
"Yes," said Coyote, "when those guys ran away on me,
those speakers of all different tongues,
whooping and hollering; only a few remained
and those ones I then dumped out too";
"How come you never listen to me?"
Sinawav asked;
"Now they will start making arrows,"
he told him, "and soon they'll be fighting you,
fighting you and me," he said;

so Coyote made arrows (preparing for war);
and later they all fought each other on the plains,
those were Comanches, and others as well . . .
all kinds of Indians
from around here, from the east,
and from that country over there (gesture);

but those few ones left (who remained in the bag)
were the Utes, the real Utes from around here;
so Sinawav said: "Those few ones,
no one will surpass them in fighting;
the Ute that is so small,
they will keep slaugthering
all the others" he said.

It was all Coyote's doing, he had done it;
and lo . . . that's the way it turned out;
that's the way it used to be,
long ago they were fighters,
this Ute, nobody could ever beat them;
they used to fight
the Comanches and everybody else,
they used to slaughter them; that's the way
he told it, that one, Sinawav,

the way he predicted; that's the way it was.
I've spoken.

3.

Now there is another *nahna adulvdi gesvi* (of that wanting which is):

According to the Ute creation story, diversity and the possibilities of meaning have another way of looking:

We came from brush cut into twigs and put into a bag. We were not to be let out while on the way to another place.

But Coyote opened the bag to look.

Now part of us is in a place we weren't intended to be.

It was Coyote who let some sticks out of the bag before he got where he was supposed to let them out.

To know the factions is the *oops* of Coyote.

We are tribes at war. Even within ourselves.

That's the way it is.

Get used to it.

We have to keep shifting so we don't take root outside of what can't be held in the space between the words:

The intrusion of *other* into the text.

Or the text into the *other*.

To stay in the bag until it reaches its destination of understanding.

Its placement in open country.

Its grounding in space.

Headwind

In China they have no religion. No Bible-Belt religion like I know, anyway. Or I don't think they do. Or that's what I heard somewhere. If I lived in China, I would not have been able to walk on air the morning the pilot said they got a write up on a taillight when they came in last night and it didn't get taken care of, and now we're waiting on the mechanic to come from the other side of the Birmingham airport and it may take a while, and I feel the sludge of the day unfold.

At the start of the overnight trip, in Minneapolis yesterday, I waited in a long line while only four stations were open at the Northwest check in counter that holds at least twelve stations, and the trip was already as disappointing as Northwest à la carte food and just as predictable. But I got to Birmingham after a plane change in Memphis, and now I return with a possible connection missed and a ride from the airport wondering what happened, and have my absence at a meeting to explain, when I want to move from the gate and the frustration of delay and the carelessness of the airline company while I read their executives on the list of millionaires in the newspaper with not enough people at the check in counter and eight stations closed because it saves money and that is the capitalism I've always stood up for.

On the last Northwest trip, I was seven hours on the plane with a bag of peanuts. The plane sat on the runway before takeoff, waiting with the back door open in the heat when the auxilliary shut down, and we listened to the planes roar by. Finally, the plane was towed back to the gate. And after the long wait for repairs, we returned to the runway to try again.

And because I'm not in China where I heard they have no Bible-

Belt Christian-fundamentalist religion, where they could not separate the plane from its gate in prayer to Jesus, where they do not know the God who opens up heaven to the planes, I can try to reach the heaven my religion knows.

I got up at 5:45 to sit in a plane with a taillight that could have been replaced last night, or at least when the plane was boarding, and not when they backed from the gate, saying, wait, there's no taillight, and the mechanic is on the other side of the airport, on the other side of the world in China where they have no born-again religion. And I would not have Jesus to pray to. I assume so, anyway. But because in America I do, the flight, finally, is bumpy, with fog below us among the rivers.

We move over Birmingham on Northwest flight 630. The hills are full of green trees, and the suburbs and highway, the pattern of quarries, and the silos of what looks like a nuclear power plant. And there is still fog between the hills.

The line of clouds in the distance could also be called fog, because they look alike, only they have different names being denser and higher up, but still they are the same white sheet over the Tennessee Valley as we approach Memphis to try to catch a plane to MSP, if we're not too late. The highways get thicker, and the houses show up, and my ears feel full of air that should not be clumped where I see the fog lifting into clouds.

In China they have no Bible-Belt Christian-fundamentalist born-again Holy-Spirit religion, and I think, who would I thank for my rice bowl, and who would I ask to bless my rice fields? What would I do with the sense of sadness? Loss? Grief? Maybe there are household gods there. Maybe China has something for its god, and if they don't, who will temper them when they wake as a nation? Who will be their consciousness? What will their conscience be?

And where did I hear China didn't have any evangelical Christian religion like I know, anyway? Maybe a missionary who went there and failed.

The landing flaps go down over brown squares of fields, the blue-green hills, and the two-bell signal from the captain rings like a church bell as the plane rumbles down to the earth, and the trees reach up for the embrace.

The flight attendant says we aren't late in arriving, but we are, as if saying it could change the fact. And maybe the hands of the clock move differently for them, having millionaires at the top of their company hiking up the prices of Northwest tickets and skimming off what those behind the check in counters could be earning.

And how can I read my own story when God is the setter of limits? It's his way and not my own. Yet there's room for my way too. Whatever I have faith for, I can speak into existence. *As your faith so it is according to you.* — Matthew 9:29. In other words, what I believe is what I have. Well, I can make an avenue for it to happen and not a roadblock.

Maybe that's the difference.

So the attendant can say the flight isn't late and she has a right to say it.

The planes look quiet in their gates, but I see those turbos or wind tunnels under the wings, whatever they are called, they look like udders, and that hole in the end of the plane, and I think of the intake of air when they're up there, a flock of birds wouldn't have a chance, and I hear the roar of another resurrection as a plane reaches the air.

In China they have no four-square religion, and the next flight leaves from gate B2 after I arrive at B41, and the attendant says it isn't far, and I have a carry-on bag, a small one for overnight, and the next plane is nearly wiggling from its gate, and I run before the thrust that will lift it from its cross of runways.

Hallelujah, I run for my turn to dance.

In China they have no evangelical four-square down-home religion, but in America, I pass the B gates of lower numbers, the corridor between them long as flight. The waiting area at B2 is empty when I arrive, but the door to the walkway is still open, the plane still at the gate. A Northwest non-millionaire checks my ticket and I am in the tunnel and on the plane facing people as I walk to my seat and find a place to stow my bag. But now, I am sitting on the plane that turns, stops, and I feel the power and know this takeoff is what I am meant to do.

The fields grow farther away into the road and I know I am in flight.

The homebound flight is longer because of headwinds, the pilot says. Even the flight is a train uphill, and I hear the engine chug, and the headwinds I don't see, bullying the plane, standing in the way when I want to get by. The pilot says it's thirty-one degrees in Minneapolis and I hear it's turned winter while I was gone overnight.

The clouds below us look like rice paddies. The interstate is a great wall. That's what I know about China. They have ducks there too. And bicycles. And order.

The pilot says we're taking a cold wind on the nose, over a hundred miles an hour. I think of him in the cockpit with his earflaps and fur-collared jacket, and in a corner of the window, there's a fighter formation of frost I usually don't see 'til midwinter, and we're not even halfway through October.

At MSP, the heavy plane touches down with hardly a jar. Sometimes they get it right, like a spread of language I hear behind me, someone probably from Alabama, and I listen to his lull as we come to earth and I see the runway streaked with black rubber marks.

And there is my waiting ride, back to my house, back to the mail and the calls, back to meetings and classes.

Walking past the Northwest check in counter on my way to the door, I see the long line again. Maybe Northwest wants the line backed up to show there's a backed up line, so it will look like more people fly Northwest than other airlines, in Minnesota anyway.

But in America, I have my religion, which is a runway in any open field that has space and hope and charity where you give as you drive out of the parking lot.

On Boards and Broken Pieces of the Ship

which consists of three parts

1.

My Thoughts on God

2.

*Some Thoughts on the Lakota Religion
from Black Elk's* The Sacred Pipe
(since I'm in Dakota/Lakota Territory)

3.

Some Afterthoughts

*I went to America to convert the Indians,
but who will convert me? — John Wesley*

1.

I remember driving one night in Texas when tumbleweeds blew
across the road. It was like driving through a kangaroo herd, the way
the tumbleweeds jumped in the headlights. Sometimes they'd hit the
car and I'd brace myself for the impact, but they tumbled over.

As I read Karen Armstrong's *History of God* (Ballantine, 1993), I
remembered the tumbleweeds, because the diversity and complexities
of ideas, opinions, options, possibilities, interpretations, and interpola-
tions of God, rolled across the road. Each page was a tumbleweed.
Each paragraph was a tumbleweed.

And I am going to add more — the Native American view of God,
which is just as diverse and filled with possibilities as the book. Native
Americans have differing views of God. The different tribes and mixed
bloods of those tribes have unique cultures, and within those cultures, within families, there's a multitude and a mixture of beliefs and
practices.

First of all, I want to say that many Native Americans are Christians.
Catholics, Baptists, all denominations are probably represented. And
certainly, many Native Americans reject Christianity. And it would

be fair to say that many Native Americans who are Christians mix Christianity with traditional ways, and walk in both worlds.

When Giles Gamble, a colleague in the English Department, read *Klondike Fever* by Pierre Berton (New York: Knopf, 1958), he found a passage he shared with me. In talking about the Tlingit who worked as packers during the Alaskan gold rush, Berton said, "Constant communion with the whites had made them shrewd bargainers. They worked for the highest bidder, ran their own informal union, and refused to labor on Sundays (for all were strict Presbyterians)." (p. 245)

In talking about the Native American culture, in talking about their concept of God, or anyone's concept of God, for that matter, I feel like I'm talking about something that cannot be talked about clearly, because it goes everywhere and is everything. Like driving through tumbleweeds.

Like explaining a migrating herd of tumbleweeds, which was really like kangaroos, which are not on the open range, maybe some in zoos. But the idea of driving through an experience you really can't explain on its own terms, but seeing something other than what could be grasped, you use it, as if being able to grasp.

I have a tumbleweed in my garage and one in my basement. I took them from Oklahoma. They catch in the fences beside the highways. When I knew I was going to move to Minnesota, I stopped beside the highway and carried them to the car, in view of passing traffic. There were pieces of tumbleweed all over the car. When I moved to Minnesota, I wrapped them in sheets and put them in the U-Haul because it's messy to move tumbleweeds.

It's messy to talk about God.

But to hear the options is maybe what education is about.

I will have trouble explaining the Cherokee concept of God. My own tribe with a broken history. Uprooted by an eighteenth-century smallpox epidemic in which probably half of the Cherokee nation died, and the nineteenth-century division between east and west after the Trail of Tears.

There was an early belief that the Cherokees (and probably other Indians) were a lost tribe of Israel, because of their belief in one God, along with a few other, mostly imagined, connections. But the Cherokee concept of one God is not meaningful for me. It's abstract and remote. I think the core has been lost, because of erasure.

What Cherokee spirituality is, is a system of sacred utterances, chants, and prayers that access the spirit world, or the above world, called *Galunlati*, in which the spirits dwelled, and many spirits that are accessed are animal spirits and ghosts beings, rather than God.

The sacred realm was the sky. It was a *rock sky* on which animals used to live but fell off to the water below, and formed mud on the surface, out of which land grew. Which was called Turtle Island. Which became America.

So Cherokee religion was a series of utterances to invoke power. The blue sparrow hawk could be called on to combat disease brought on by other winged creatures. The white beaver would help you cross water.

If we didn't honor them, the animals could inflict *Ool-skay-tah* on us, which is disease, distress, anguish, and death. There are stories of the animals talking about the cruelty of men. Disease was their revenge, which they also could heal.

That there was something wrong with us that needed to be healed was a basic concept. And there were powerful sacred chants that certain people could use. It was fearful. Superstitious. Something that could go either way.

Like the Dakotas-Lakotas, the Cherokees had to make tobacco and smoke offerings and be careful not to offend any animal. And since the animals were killed for food and clothing, there was a danger to life.

I want to say there was a sense of the Old Testament God of anger and revenge who had certain holy men, and you took your offering to them and asked for intercession. I guess that's another source of the "lost tribe of Israel" idea.

Some of the old ways are still practiced in rural eastern Oklahoma. There's the Redbird Smith Keetowah society. But often, you find Cherokees at the Baptist church on Sundays.

For the Cherokees, it is still the power of the word, which is why Christianity came easy, especially when Christ is described as the Word.

That and a sense of something being wrong with man, and therefore, being in need of a savior.

I could understand that Christ as a spirit became flesh and drew my sins into him when he was destroyed on the cross, and through faith, I could be healed of my sins and sicknesses, understanding through the apostle Paul that I still have sin as long as I am in the body of flesh, but eventually in the afterworld, I would somehow be like Christ, or at least be with him. And certainly the Bible is open to interpretation. Just look at Christianity alone for a myriad of denominations and fractures within those denominations.

Many times, the Indians asked, *how can we believe in a God the white man can't agree on?*

Nonetheless, I could hold onto the thought that Christ became flesh, got himself in alignment with us, shifted our sins to himself. God judged him. He died. He came back to life. Now we are aligned with him. We have access to the godhead.

Sin is my willful separation from that belief.

I have need of faith. I could not believe in nothing. The Native American has a sense of spirit, and I had to grasp some ideas. I had to have something I could relate to. I was born during the Holocaust, and though I couldn't read the newspaper, it stuck to everyone. There was the atomic bomb of 1945. Korea. Vietnam. I lived in a messy world, and America had its fingers everywhere. We were implicated in what went on.

We live in this world, my father told me.

When I was growing up, I had a sense of blood and death and injustice, as well as life and hope and goodness. My father was a Cherokee man without education. He came from the backroads of Arkansas, and through work and responsiblity became plant superintendent at Armour's in Kansas City. There was a time those things happened. Maybe they still do. My Cherokee grandmother was illiterate, and I make my living reading and teaching and writing.

When I was a girl, we went to Trinity Methodist Church in Kansas City. One should try to be a good person, like Christ, and there was a sense of brotherhood while attending church.

But, for me, there had to be more than that. There had to be power. I couldn't be good on my own.

When I was in Kansas City, this past Christmas, I drove through my old neighborhood, which is now inner city. I passed the Baptist church at 50th and Garfield where I was sent to vacation Bible school as a child, and heard about Jesus, who came seeking the lost sheep and entered my life with the power of the spirit world.

His father was a many-faced God. Fierce, yet loving. Personal, yet beyond the grasp of the human mind.

In the Bible, I later learned, there were different accounts of creation, of the flood. There were discrepencies, inconsistencies, contradictions, ambiguities.

But the Old Testament said, *My ways are not your ways* — Isaiah 55:8, and it was understood that God worked the way God worked.

It is that God, that belief system, the born-again church, I have held onto most of my life.

I can read statements in Armstrong's *History of God* such as Christ died on the cross to wake our compassion so that we might be better people. Or the statement that Jesus in the gospels never said he came to atone for sin, nor wanted to found a godly state, and his mission failed and he died in despair.

And I still believe.

I know the darker parts of Christian history. The church sold pardons. There were inquisitions. Witch burnings.

God still seems unable to make up his mind whether he serves judgment or grace.

There are some downright unacceptable passages in the Bible. *Let your women keep silence in the churches; for it is not permitted unto them to speak, but they should be commanded to be under obedience. And if they will learn anything, let them ask their husbands at home.* — I Corinthians 14:34–35.

There's an exclusionary attitude in Christian fundamentalists.

Who needs it? I could think.

Yet I've had a born-again experience.

2.

Now, since I am in the Dakota-Lakota northern plains territory, I want to look at their religious ceremonies. It's a culture I'm not from, but I've looked at it as an outsider.

Since Christianity uses the Jewish territory of the Old Testament, I can witness other Native American traditions, such as the sweat lodge and Sun Dance. Their tobacco prayer ties, using black for west, red for north, yellow for east, and white for south, are sometimes part of my prayers.

The passages I quote are taken from *The Sacred Pipe, Black Elk's Account of the Seven Rites of the Oglala Sioux* (or Lakota), recorded in 1947 when Black Elk was 85 years old by Joseph Epes Brown (Norman: University of Oklahoma Press, 1989).

[These are the visions that] came to me in my youth. . . . We have been told by the white man, or at least those who are Christian, God sent to man his son who would restore peace and order upon the earth; and we have been told that Jesus the Christ was crucified, but that he shall come again at the Last Judgment, the end of this world or cycle. This I understand and know it is true, but the white man should know too, that it was the will of *Wakan Tanka*, the Great Spirit, that an animal turn itself into a two-legged person in order to bring the most holy pipe to His People; and we too were taught that White Buffalo Calf Woman who brought the sacred pipe will appear again at the end of this world, a coming which we Indians know is not far off.

Most people call it a peace pipe, yet we know there is not peace in the world or even between neighbors. . . . There is much talk of peace among the Christians, yet this is just talk. Perhaps it may be, and this is my prayer that, through our sacred pipe, and through this book, peace may come to those peoples who can understand, an understanding which must be of the heart and not the head. . . .

We should understand that all things are the work of the Great Spirit. . . . He is within all things: the trees, grasses, the rivers, mountains, and all the four-legged animals, and the winged peoples; and even more important, we should understand that He is also above all these things and peoples. When we understand [with] our hearts, then we will . . . be and act and live as He intends. (from the foreword) . . .

Many winters ago, two Lakota were hunting, . . . and as they were standing on a hill looking for game, they saw in the distance something coming toward them. [It was a woman] dressed in white buckskin, and bearing a bundle on her back. One of the Lakota had bad intentions and told his friend of his desire, but the other man said that he must not have such thoughts, for surely this was a *wakan*, [or spirit] woman. [She] was now close to the men, and putting down her bundle, she asked the one with bad intentions to come to her. As the young man approached, . . . they were both covered by a cloud, and soon when it lifted the sacred woman was standing there, and at her feet was the man with the bad thoughts who was now nothing but bones, and terrible snakes were eating him. (3–4)

The White Buffalo Calf Woman told the other man to return to his chief and tell him to prepare a large teepee in which he should gather all his people.

When they had gathered, the *wakan* woman took the pipe from the bundle she carried. Holding the pipe up with its stem to the heavens, she said,

With this sacred pipe you will walk upon the Earth; for the Earth is your Grandmother and Mother, and She is sacred. Every step that is taken upon her should be a prayer. The bowl of the pipe is red stone; it is the Earth. . . . The stem of the pipe is wood, and this represents all that grows upon the Earth. [The] twelve feathers which hang from the stem [are from the] Spotted Eagle, and they represent all the wingeds of the air. All the people and all the things of the universe, are joined to you who smoke the pipe. (5–6)

She then told them about seven ceremonies that they should follow. The pipe was to be used in all of them. It is central to the Lakota religion. It was the coming of Christ to them, full of ceremony and order and a certain way of doing things.

1. *Keeping of the Soul,* a wake of sorts, in which the body is wrapped in a bundle and placed on a scaffolding. (10–30)

2. *Purification,* the *inipi* or sweat lodge, which a small tent filled with heat where participants make prayer and intercession.

> The [*inipi*] utilizes all the Powers of the universe: earth, water, fire and air. The sweat lodge is made from twelve young willows, [bent to form a rounded framework, which was covered with buffalo hides (but now, with blankets and tarps)]. The willows. . . are set in such a way to mark the four quarters of the universe, thus, the whole lodge is the universe in an image, and the two legged, four legged, and winged people, and all things of the world, are contained within, it, for the people and things too must be purified before they can send a voice to *Wakan Tanka* [the Great Spirit]. (31–32)

Rocks are heated in a fire outside the sweat lodge. They are carried in and placed in a pit in the center. The flap door is closed. Water is poured over the rocks, and the sweat lodge is filled with heat.

> Oh Grandfather and Father *Wakan Tanka,* maker of all that is, who always has been, behold me! And you, Grandmother and Mother Earth, You are *wakan* and have holy ears; hear me! We have come from You, we are a part of You, and we know that our bodies will return to You at that time when our spirits travel up the great path. By fixing this center in the earth, I remember You to whom my body will return, but above all, I think of *Wakan Tanka*, with whom our spirits become as one. By purifying myself in this way, I wish to make myself worthy of you, O *Wakan Tanka*, that my people may live! (33–34)

> I am sending a voice. . . . Hear me, . . . *Wakan Tanka*, Grandfather, You are first and always have been. You have brought us to

this great island, and here our people wish to live in a sacred manner. Teach us to know and to see all the powers of the universe, and give to us the knowledge to understand that they are all really one Power. May our people always send their voices to You as they walk the sacred path of life! (37)

Then the pipe is passed around and another of the four rounds begin. Since I live in the north, I will quote the prayer for that direction.

Behold, O you Baldheaded Eagle, there where the giant *Waziah* has his lodge! *Wakan Tanka* has paced you there to control this path; you are there to guard the health of the people, that they may live. Help us with your cleansing wind! May it make us pure so that we may walk the sacred path in a holy manner. . . . O *Wakan Tanka,* Grandfather, above all, it is Thy will we are doing here. Through the Power which comes from the place where the giant *Waziah*, lives, we are now making ourselves as pure and as white as the snow. We know that we are now in darkness, but soon the Light will come. When we leave this lodge . . . may we be as children newly born! May we live again, O *Wakan Tanka.* (40)

The door of the lodge is then opened, . . . representing the coming of the purifying Power of the north, and also we see the light which destroys darkness, just as wisdom drives away ignorance. (38–40)

Water is then passed to the leader, who offers it to the men, and another round begins.

[The *inipi* or sweat lodge is] used before any undertaking for which we wish to make ourselves pure, or for which we wish to gain strength; and in many winters past, our men, and often the women, made the *inipi* even every day, and sometimes several times a day, and from this we receive much of our power. Now that we have neglected these rites we have lost much of our power; it is not good, and I cry when I think of it. (43)

The other ceremonies are:

3. *Vision Quest*, where the seeker goes up on the hill and stays in isolation for up to four days. Through fasting and prayer, he receives the wisdom he seeks.

There is a purification lodge before the vision quest or lamentation.

> In a sacred manner you must gather the rocks and sage, and then you must make a bundle of five long sticks and also five bundles of twelve small sticks, all of which will be used as offerings. These sticks you should lean against the west side of the sweat lodge until we are ready to purify them. We shall also need the Ree twist tobacco, kinnikinnik, a tobacco cutting board, buckskin for the tobacco offering bags, sweet grass, a bag of sacred earth, a knife, and a stone hatchet. (48)

As I read these, they sound like ingredients for a recipe. But more, I am reminded of the offerings for the tabernacle in the Old Testament.

> In the tobacco offerings, the Lord said to Moses, Take unto thee sweet spices with frankincense, temper it together pure and holy. And thou shalt beat some of it very small and put of it before the testimony in the tabernacle of the congregation, where I will meet with thee: it shall be unto you most holy. (Exodus 30:34–36)

4. *Sun Dance*, which I have discussed in its own essay.

5. *Making of Relatives*, a relationship between peoples of other tribes. (101–115)

6. *Rite of Passage for a Young Woman*, a prayer and purification ceremony that takes place after the first menstrual cycle. It honors the young woman as a *tree of life*. In part of the ceremony, the young woman takes four sips from a bowl of water in which cherries are floating. (116–126)

7. *The Throwing of the Ball*, of which Black Elk says

> [The game represents the course of a man's life, which should be spent in trying to get the ball, for the ball represents *Wakan Tanka*, or the universe. The ball is] made from the hair of a buffalo and

covered with tanned buffalo hide. [It is painted] red, the color of the world, and at the four quarters, [blue dots are painted for the heavens]; then two blue circles [are painted], running all around the ball, thus making two paths joining the four quarters. By completely encircling the red ball with blue lines, Heaven and Earth were united into one in this ball, thus making it very sacred. (132)

A young woman then holds the ball.

O Grandfather, Father, *Wakan Tanka*, behold us! [The young woman holds] the universe in her hand. Upon that earth all who move will rejoice this day. The four powers of the universe and also the sacred heaven are there with the ball. [The young woman] sees the generations to come and the tree of life at the center. . . . She sees her Grandmother and Mother Earth and all her relatives in the things that move and grow. She stands there with the universe in her hand, and all her relatives are really one. (133)

Then the ball was thrown and there was a great scramble until finally one person had the ball and returned it to the young woman at the center.

3.

Again, I remember driving through Texas at night, and the herd of tumbleweeds crossing my headlights and some of them hitting the car. They are short, stubby bushes that break off from the ground and roll in the wind, and there is a lot of wind and a lot of tumbleweed on the southern plains, and there's a lot of ways to believe in God, or not believe, in the enormity of our history.

Somehow, in the Judeo-Christian heritage, God made known how to approach him. Adam and Eve in the garden tried to cover themselves with leaves, but God clothed their nakedness with animal skin. That was the first shedding of blood. Then Cain brought the harvest of his hand and was rejected, but Abel brought wine, which was used to symbolize blood. Not by my own works, but God made a way. Cain was so angry about this that he killed his brother. But the way of the blood prevailed.

The same thought is echoed later, in the fortieth chapter of Genesis, when the butler and baker have dreams in Pharaoh's prison. The butler dreamed of a cluster of grapes that he pressed into a cup. The baker dreamed of baskets of baked goods. Joseph interpreted their dreams for them. He told the butler he would live and he told the baker he would not.

I think of the Lakota who saw the White Buffalo Calf Woman in the wrong way and turned to bones. The other recognized her as a *wakan*, a spirit, and received what she had to say.

Again, I think of all the ways Karen Armstrong approaches God through history.

For me, Jesus was the utterance invoked by the spirit world. I can pray to him without a holy man or priest between us. My act of faith is voluble. Moveable. Rollable. But facing the hard economic wall of this world and the uncertainties of life by myself, the options rolled over and over like tumbleweed, and in some of them, I found substance and stability, something not inflexible, to meet a myriad of needs as I drove my car down the highway of life.

I could even head north from Oklahoma where I'd lived my adult life, to face the rigors of the Minnesota winters and academia, which was a territory where no one in my family had been, and where I had no one but myself to take with me.

For the Native American, life is difficult, uncertain, confusing and full of pit stops. It may be that way for others. It seems to me, without belief or faith in something, it's like crossing the country without a map, or facing an interchange without road markers, so you don't know which way to turn to get where you want to go.

Possibly, we're all looking for transcendence. For the traditional Indian, it's doing things in a certain way. Black Elk's *The Sacred Pipe* is full of exact and minute details, and if they weren't followed strictly, something bad could happen. A serpent could wrap itself around your leg. And in this day, you could say it's the snake of alcoholism and uncenteredness.

The problem with Indian ritual, it seems to me, is that it doesn't survive the circumstances in which it exists. There has to be transcendence. Otherwise, there is a huge gulf between God and man which something had to bridge.

The Bible is acceptable to me because it's a story told by many voices and many versions. The book of Hebrews begins *God, who at sundry times and in divers manners spake in time past.*

I want a story that is a house in my heart. I want to be a New Testament Indian released of all those duties. I want this absurd religion, Christianity, which fits the absurdity of the human race.

Christianity has always been a resister of definition, a problematic religion with controversy, disagreement and many interpretations. Yet, I don't want to be like Jacob, who said, *God is in this place and I never knew it* — Genesis 28:16. I want to hear the Great Spirit in the noise of the birds at my feeder. I have a long board across the corner of a fence in my yard, and when something scares them, I hear them take off with the hum of their wings.

In that terrible storm in Acts, chapter twenty-seven, verse forty-four, when the apostle Paul and others on the ship had been tossed in the sea for fourteen days and nights, Paul stood in the middle of them and said, *Be of good cheer*, while the ship was being torn apart close to shore. Those who could swim, did. *And the rest, some on boards and some on broken pieces of the ship.* And so it came to pass that they all escaped safely to the land.

I see the Indian nations as the ship broken apart on the rocks, but the pieces are still there. God also could be a ship the storm of humanity has torn into many pieces, but I found my pieces to hold onto because otherwise, I would drown.

In the end, I can accept an uncertain, contradictory, changing-yet-unchanging God, full of passion, calmness, and a certain practicality.

Why Nations War

Vengeance is mine . . . saith the Lord.
—Romans 12:19

August 28. It's 4:00 in the morning and I'm at my desk. Across the alley, just behind my house, is Rosemark Bakery. Each night, they load six delivery trucks, banging metal racks, pulling down the rear doors.

After they load, they drive through the alley, turn, and drive up my street where they have parked their cars. They stop in front of my house, unload donut boxes into the trunks of their cars, bang their trunks and the door of the trucks, and drive off with the sound of their diesel engines.

But this morning, there're also delivery trucks in the alley. Dawn Bakery Supply, an 18-wheeler, unloads its heavy sacks of baking supplies, leaving the motor of the truck and the refrigeration unit running. They are supposed to unload during the day, because it's the law. Often they move in at night.

There are city ordinances against noise (Chapter 293, Sections 293.06 and 293.09, Numbers 16915 and 17448) prohibiting deliveries between 11:00 PM and 7:00 AM. I think Rosemark Bakery has broken every ordinance. I find old letters of complaint in my word processor. I find grievances written on the stone tablets of my ears.

Over the years, they rattle the neighborhood. They rattle nations.

I looked at houses three years before I found the little house behind the bakery, paying more than I should have because I didn't know to offer less than the asking price. It was the first house I bought.

The first time I saw the man who sold me the house, after I moved in, he asked how I was getting along with the bakery. I'd already picked up their wrapping papers and order forms from my yard. I should have known.

But I refinanced when the interest rates went down. I redecorated. I can walk to work. In the middle of a Minnesota winter, I don't have to get my car out of the garage. I've called the mayor's complaint line over the years. I've called the councilman's office. Nothing has worked. When I'm not teaching, I write at my desk just a few yards from the bakery.

Once, midwinter, when the bakery was using a forklift for a snow plow at 3:00 in the morning, I called the police. Soon, a policeman knocked on my door in the dark and asked what I wanted him to do. He said I was the only one who complained. He went behind my house to the bakery, probably commiserating with the men who had to work at night, probably finding camaraderie, agreeing about a complaining woman. Later, the policeman drove away in his rounded Chevrolet police car that looked like a loaf of bread. Later, the snow plowing continued.

The next morning at 7:00 AM, when I had gone back to sleep, another policeman called and said if there was anything else they could do, just call.

Well, there're other businesses on either side of them, and a parking lot on one side of my house. Who else is there for them to wake?

After they load their trucks behind the bakery, and unload whatever they unload in front of my house, and drive off to unload wherever they unload their trucks after that, they go to their houses to bed. But I live in the middle of a twenty-four-hour business. During the day, I have delivery trucks blocking the alley in front of my garage. B&B also is an 18-wheeler, and Fleischmann's, a smaller truck that also leaves its motor and refrigeration unit running while it unloads. Then there's Dawes Transport delivering Bak-Krisp and all the other trucks bringing their wares, their oil and leavening, their mixing bowls, dough boards, and kneading toughs.

The largest truck at the bakery is the flour-delivery truck from Buesing Transport, a shiny steel 18-wheeler. It takes two hours to force the flour through a pressurized tube into the bakery. The truck makes regular deliveries every other week. My windows hum. My house rocks. Dishes on the shelves shimmy. The man beats against the sides of the giant truck with a rod to loosen the packed flour. There's a jagged buzzer that sounds.

Later, the trash-hauling trucks lift the bakery's dumpsters high in the air, shaking loose the lumps of dough, leaving the swarms of flies, the bees, larvae, and the smell of rotten eggs. At other times, the workers clack the metal dumpster lids, letting them fall from midair. The noise rattles loose the Testaments from the Bible on my desk.

> The Kenites, and the Kenizzites, and the Kadmonites,
> And the Hittites, and the Perizzites, and the Rephaim,
> And the Amorites, and the Cannanites, and the Girgashites, and the Jebusites. (Genesis 15:19–21)

All the warring tribes against Israel.

I try to ignore the bakery traffic and the assault of the Buesing trucks, but I turn furious with noise. I know what I'll feel like at the end of my work day. I have them to listen to again at night and the following days and nights. I could blast them off the earth.

I have talked to them for six years about their noise. They say there's nothing they can do. I can move or be quiet. But who would buy a house surrounded by a bakery?

Once I even called Carol Rosemark, the sweet owner of the bakery. She said if I have any ideas of how they can get supplies and load trucks without making noise, she would be glad to hear. Like the policeman, she also said she never hears complaints from anyone but me.

The bakery pokes at memories.

The metal door on the back of the bakery clangs continually, and I remember the convent bell that jarred the old neighborhood. That's what the door sounds like. That's what I want it to sound like.

When I hear the door, I want transport. I want to think of my childhood and Kansas City where I lived as a girl. I want to remember the convent up the street. Our family went to the Methodist church, and I didn't know what happened in convents. The nuns stayed behind high walls and closed gates. I imagined them shut up in their rooms under heavy canvas habits, their prayers rising like the roar of bakery trucks in the night.

Across the city, during the day, my father drove cattle up the ramp in the stockyards. In the convent, I imagined Christ sacrificed like cattle.

Now the white bakery trucks purr in the alley. They wake old terrors. The angry helplessness of childhood. Surrounded on all sides.

I feel my dreams not dreamed. Wallowing in grogginess, I know why nations war. No wonder there are bombs. In the rubble of my sleeplessness there are destroyed cities.

Bless you, Buesing truck and Rosemark Bakery, with the fury of the Lord. Bless you with his heavenly work boot. May his oven blast get you. The noise of his bakery truck pound you forever. May you know the sawmill conveyer belt. The sleeplessness without latitude.

Bless you bakery workers who park a few yards from my bedroom window at 4:00 in the morning. Gray Honda and bronze Chevrolet Corsica, hoards of lice and gnat-plagues upon you.

May the sky unload its burden of sun at vespers on your bakery rack.

And it came to pass when the sun went down, and it was dark, behold a smoking furnace, and a burning lamp. (Genesis 15:17)

It could be a DC-7 in the alley. A grandstand concert at the state fairgrounds. I prophesy one thousand Baltimore orioles perched on your bakery racks.

May all the tires on your trucks go flat.

May your toes bake forever.

May boll weevils eat your flour.

Take these warrior words. These spears. These death units. These destroyers.

I have given this land, from the river of Egypt to the river Euphrates. (Genesis 15:18)

But I feel the smallness of my human heart. I feel my rage unleash. I throw out peace. I drown forgiveness.

Level the bakery. Because of them, I acknowledge the need of atonement in my heart. Because of them, I know my fury, my taste for revenge.

High, holy bakery. All night I hear the bakery trucks pray. May Christ come from his cross.

May I walk as one who gathereth eggs that are left. (Isaiah 10:14)

At 5:30 in the morning, another 18-wheeler, *Sexton Quality Foods Since 1883 Serving Hotels–Restaurants–Institutions*, delivers.

The noise rattles loose the Jews, Catholics, Protestants, Muslims. The Cavalry. The Indians. The boundaries. War zones. The barriers of sleep.

Get the bakery, Lord.

I untie their shoe in front of the elders at the gate of the city.

May they be a bag of Fritos under Your feet.

North Shore Portrait

Is that it then? Is that the law of freedom?
That she must see him yet must not touch?
—Jorie Graham, "Noli Me Tangere"

I was on the shore of Crane Lake, several hours from Lake Superior, when I saw the northern lights for the first time. The sky was black with stars, then there was this drift of fuzzed lights. Then another. The whole sky twanged with the transparent streaks of moving, muted light. Yellow as a program for an old church service. Yellowed as wallpaper hanging in the upstairs of a vacated Minnesota farmhouse.

I was traveling on a Blandin–Private College Foundation grant with two students and a research assistant, my portable word processor plugged into the car's cigarette lighter.

I had been wondering what was the heart of the project called "North Shore Portrait." At first, I wasn't sure what to do with the project. My companions had been videotaping the landscape. Wanting to stop at every rock. Following a map given us by a colleague, Roger Blakely. I had been listening to the more distant voice of the painter, Dewey Albinson, the focus of our project, who in the earlier part of our century painted and made wood engravings of the North Shore of Lake Superior, and who saw changes in the land almost as he painted.

As we traveled north, I watched the changes still going on. There were places the land was chewed by bulldozers and tunneled by dynamite. At the same time, I had listened to the gulls and saw the fog that came each morning. I thought about conflict and resolution, the heart of every piece of writing. If it is writing.

So what would happen in the "North Shore Portrait"? Our video project about a painter, Dewey Albinson, whose story began, "When I was fourteen a neighbor gave me a box of paints," and ended with the painter so crippled by disease that he had to wheel himself on a trolley between his paintings on the floor?

The night we arrived at Grand Portage, I heard the casino noise, and the next morning, the bulldozer digging the earth for more of it, and I wanted to step off the earth, or at least back into nature. I walked up the road and picked some wildflowers, but a buzz-fly dived at my head and I swatted him away but he stuck with me, and I thought, well, nature isn't so great either.

I had talked about what to do with the project—a combination of paintings and video—of history and environment—of the voices of white and Indian—well, I wanted to step into the delicious mess that any project is at first and see what resolution we could move to. I looked for complications more than a simple plea to take care of the land. We can't go back or oversimplify. It takes technology and progress as well as conservation and stewardship for our survival.

I had watched the gulls gliding off Mt. Josephine over Lake Superior. I had watched one student videotaping the other as he came up the path as though it were the 1930s and he were Dewey Albinson himself.

I had read the pages of Albinson's journal that my research assistant, Kristi Wheeler, had excerpted. I listened to the students' insights into the project and watched them interact with the landscape and with each other. Some of my favorite times in teaching are when I become invisible and the students fly on their own.

I began to realize I wouldn't write a script for this project as I had in the other projects, but let the painter's own words from his journal speak, and the land itself would speak, and the video camera and Kristi Wheeler's supervision of taping and editing those eight tapes we would make during the trip into less than one. Then a third student would also speak as he gave voice to Albinson's words in our video of the life of Dewey Albinson.

It was a time I felt left out of the project. But I could watch the lake and the gulls, the animals and the land. The streaks of northern lights in the night sky.

The year I lived in Iowa, before I came to Minnesota, I rented a farmhouse in a row of other farmhouses just north of Interstate 80, in

Springdale, just northeast of Iowa City. It was a year that came from heaven for me like a plane landing. It was a transition year, an airport year.

The people next to me had a dog they kept fenced with the sheep. Actually, it was their son's dog. The son must have moved on and didn't want it. Once, while I was reading by the window, I saw the son come for the dog. It was the only time I saw him near it in the year I lived there. He took the dog from the sheep pasture to his truck. Probably he had to take it to the vet as punishment for not taking care of it other times.

When the son returned, the dog dug its feet into the ground to keep from being pulled to the pen. I watched the man struggle with the dog, pulling the leash as hard as he could, his own feet digging into the ground. Finally, he got the dog back into the sheep pen and closed the gate and drove off, leaving the dog at the fence, banished to its place among the sheep.

I remembered that dalmatian in Iowa under the northern lights in Minnesota. I remember it the times I stand alone with something I am not kin to, such as the lights when they are there, unlike the dalmatian, who always is when I think of him in Iowa, more than the lights.

Often my thoughts are disjointed as the dog and the streaks of light, as if someone turned into the driveway of heaven after a *dissettlement* of being, an experiential fragmentation of voice, a vision of broken narrative, an interlocking diffusionism of unclear boundaries that leads to the realization of joint property.

A dalmatian in a sheep pen unconnected to the sheep or the owners is an emblem of mixed heritage, a new American frontier.

In the end, it's hard to put my finger on. It's something I have to be in to see. It is critical faith theory: there is no objective reality but what you believe.

So you see my bias. My car lights turning into the driveway of space, stirring up the northern lights as though they were a dalmatian waiting for someone to take it from the sheepfold, as though waiting for someone who wanted it in this just universe where it must be, as though waiting for someone to recognize it as different from the sheep, or as though waiting to be noticed, to belong to someone.

I think I can say language exists because God exists. As if getting back to God. Never leaving Him alone. Changing direction until the essay floats like the northern lights. Until it is interdependent.

I can speak the form of language into being. But the process is not a one-way street. The eardrum is a womb. What I hear creates the ideas that determine actions and further forms of language.

What I hear is fundamental. *Does not the ear try words?*—Job 12:11.

God, like language, like the northern lights, is a mixture of weavings, raveling and unraveling, changing and contradicting, a mystery, a relativity, a multiplicity of voices and versions, a floating fictive, a context of relationships. There's an indeterminacy in the northern lights. Who can say their exact meaning? Who can touch them? Have they not spawned interpretation after interpretation? Denomination after denomination? Could they be a living, changing, moving being?

Likewise, who can say what language is, or what God is, and how they work? Are they not just as changing?

The surest way to defeat a people is to take away their language, which is not only the words but the thought-structures behind them, the life-breath of sound. Leave them like a dalmatian in a sheep pen by the fence.

When God himself wanted to diffuse power, he used himself. The way DNA makes protein, which is necessary to make more DNA.

Changing language into languages.

But now I was on a project funded by a Blandin–Private College Foundation grant. I was looking at Dewey Albinson's wood engraving *Lake Superior Fish Houses*. His sky furrowed as fields on the rolling prairie. His hills were waves on the lake. The curving wood boards of his rowboats and the walls of his cabins were as plowed as his sky. His trees were small clouds. Or volcanoes. Small vol(canoes). Puffing from the Minnesota north shore to float in a wavy sky.

I felt the engraving of his stubbornness. *I've come this far and I won't*

Dewey Albinson, *Lake Superior Fish Houses,* wood engraving, 1920s. From the collection of the Minnesota Historical Society.

back down. I acknowledge my losses and will survive by myself in a sheep pasture, if need be.

Even when nothing, as yet, is clear under the sky. Where the northern lights move like Albinson's trolley between canvases.

And far away, in a sheep pasture in Iowa. A dalmatian unable to be one with the sky. Left behind on the earth while the amazing lights flashed.

I will think of the determination that enables. Later—the two days I drive 991 miles to my son's house in Texas over spring break, the two days I drive back to Minnesota.

The years after I move somewhere I'm not from. Where it's a different somewhere than where I'm from. Wherever it is I'm from.

After the years I live alone.

After the "voice blanket" of words. Wondering what sense it makes.

Where it's going. What it drags with it from behind. Where the tares are among the wheat. And what the wheat.

The spirit, which is postmodern.
The northern sky, which is a dalmatian.

As if George Catlin's painting of a man hanging by his chest were the Sun Dance.
As if the white cones at the Denver airport were the teepees of an Indian village.
As if denominations were the act of God.

The lights are a cartography. Pointing virtual energy fields. Aurora borealis.
The lights spurt the dark night. For the lonelinesses of the road. For the cold-and-hunger dance.
The earth's magnetic pole catches electrical discharges from the sun. When there's a dusting of the sun's particles. Lighting molecules to luminosity. Igniting gases in the air. Or something like that. Which flocks the earth's polar gravity.

*   *   *

I could say Christ is multifold. I can say without Christ there is no light. Without Christ there is no Christ light. If that's the light I want. If all other forms of light are darkness according to Christ.
I can say these northern lights are tongues. I can see them running as fields from the row of farmhouses in Springdale to Interstate 80 just northeast of Iowa City.
They move in the landscape of the will in the regeneration that comes from the determination to survive.

The female cardinal outside my window is building her nest in the bush with twigs and bits of that waxy paper from the bakery across the alley.

A Ute Sun Dance Story

Told by Mollie Cloud

this is about the Sun Dance, it was long time ago;
there were two of them, an old man and an old woman,
she was his mother, the one who acted as his mother;
and he was lonely, the young man was,
without relatives; they had all perished (in an
epidemic); so he would just hunt around,
he went hunting, wandering around,
through the cedar-grown country, it was around
Mancos Creek long time ago;

   so as he hunted around, he didn't kill (anything),
he didn't kill any deer; so the next day
he went out again, having killed no deer (the day
before), he again went hunting; and once again
he returned (empty handed);

   so then . . . he became very lonely; he . . .
had no relatives; so then later on
he brooded, and he became lonely; so he decided
to kill himself, to shoot himself
in the head, right there on the rocky slope;
he was sitting on a rocky hillside, he was going
to kill himself;

   so then, having not yet loaded his gun,
all of a sudden an owl hooted right
behind him; he had hobbled his horse . . .

where he had hobbled it . . . right behind it there
it cried;

so he quit trying to kill himself,
sitting there on the slope, sitting on the rocky
hillside; then all of a sudden, for whatever reason,
he got angry; "Why is it" he said, "that
the owl is calling me? So that I shouldn't
kill myself!" he said, he thought;

then his horse . . . (the owl) kept hooting
toward where his horse was, the owl did;
when he was sitting, when he was sitting, right
behind him, it hooted; and it kept leading him
toward the horse, it kept hooting;
he had hobbled his horse quite a distance back;

so then, while he was sitting . . . I mean . . .
he stepped (up on) his horse; then all of a sudden
his . . . he mounted it and turned back,
going home; it was very far; then
when he arrived, he told his Grandmother: "Being so
lonely, I almost killed myself" he said,
"because I was so lonely" he said;
"Why are you so lonely?" asked his Grandmother,
"I'm still around,
you shouldn't do it!" she said;

well, the next day he went out again;
he had a dream in his sleep (that night),
of a deer going that way, across the rocky mesa . . .
it was a flat rocky mesa . . .

so (going across that country) there were
indeed tracks, of a deer
going across the rocky mesa; then, the young man
thought, someone was whistling right there;
there was a small arroyo there,

and suddenly from across it, there was a whistling;
so he looked that way,
he kept tracking the deer, its spoor; and right there
(in front of him) there was a White-Man standing,
on a white horse,
all dressed in white; it was a White-Man;
"What manner of dress is that?" the Young Man thought;
"it must be the White-Man's way" he thought;
so he stood and looked at him, and the White-Man
called him: "Come here!"
he told him; so the Young Man
approached slowly; and the White-Man spoke
to him then;

   he spoke in all languages . . . then . . .
heee . . . he spoke English (first), next
he spoke Spanish, but the Young Man didn't
understand . . . he then spoke (in the languages of)
all the languages of people who live on earth,
he spoke all of them;

   finally he spoke to him in his own
Ute language, finally,
but before that he spoke to him in Navajo . . .
and that the Young Man understood;
what the White-Man spoke last was Ute,
and the Young Man understood it;

   now the White-Man showed him . . .
he showed him . . . he showed him
his hand where he
had been nailed . . . and his ribs where
he had been stabbed; "How come you are like that?"
the Young Man asked; he was indeed a whole person . . .
there was nothing . . . there was nothing missing
about him;

   the Young Man himself was sort of an orphan . . .

he understood (only) when the White-Man spoke Navajo,
or in Ute; he didn't understand any
English; and he didn't know anything about it,
that this was the White-Man who had been nailed
(to the cross) on the hillside;
of what the White-Man told him
he knew nothing; "Who is this one?"
he wondered; and indeed, it was Jesus,
it was Him, He was bearded,
He had long hair.

   well then . . . the story goes . . .
"I will talk to you now" Jesus said,
"about this business yesterday of you wanting
to shoot yourself in the head" He said;
"You shouldn't do it,
even though you may be an orphan" He said then,
"I will talk to you now"
He said; "It is because of his influence
that you did it" he said;
and lo, just next to Jesus there was a Dark Man
standing, with a hook nose, like a cowboy,
just like that type, wearing a big hat,
with spurs, decked up in his finery, riding a
well-made saddle; and his horse had fierce
eyes, it was pitch black;
and lo, it was the Devil himself
it was him; so the Young Man stood and watched (him);
it was because of his power that he was going
to shoot himself
in the head (the day before);
that's what Jesus told him;

   the Young Man was scared, watching the Devil,
Jesus showed him to him; then (he said):
"I am the one who stopped you (from killing
yourself), disguised as an owl,

I'm the one who hooted at you,
I'm the one who led you away"
He told him then; so the Young Man said: "Yes"
he said, "I was feeling very
dejected when I did it"
he said, "that's why I (tried to) do it"
he told Him, the Young Ute told Jesus;

    so Jesus told him: "I will now tell you"
He said, "you . . . you . . .
'I'm lonely' that's what you said" He said;
"Now I'll show you your relatives;
your relatives are indeed alive,
your older brother" He said, "is standing
right there" He said,
"indeed I've brought him here" He said;

    and lo, right alongside Jesus
there was a person standing,
his older brother; so the Young Man stood there
looking at him; "Alright" asked Jesus,
"do you recognize him?"
He asked; "Yes, he's my older brother"
said the Young Man, "and he's been dead
for a long time";
"No" Jesus told him, "he's not dead,
he's alive, up in heaven, up there above the earth;
He said, "he's alive there,
(together with) many others"; that's what
He told him, He told him;

    then Jesus continued: "Yes" He said,
"he just came to see you, because you
were lonely, you said so yourself; now he
knows where you live" He said;
so the Young Man said: "Alright" he said,
"it's alright by me" he said;

then Jesus said: "Now I am going
to tell you the story" He said,
"of this land, the way it is going to be
in the future" He said; "right now I . . .
right now all this land is
full of Indians; but just like that (it will fill
with) whites" he said; "They'll speak all (kinds of)
languages, it will all be mixed" He said,
telling him the story; "And these
churchgoers, there'll be all kinds, there'll be
all kinds, a jumble of congregations with all kinds
of names . . . churchgoers . . . "
He said; "They'll have (different) names,
those congregations" He said; "And as to these
Indians, the ones here now, the Indians, they'll
become this way too;
now, here standing (next to you)
is the one you were longing for" He said;
"So what will become of you now?
These Indians (around you), they don't . . .
understand (about all this)" Jesus continued;
"So . . . you . . . we-two will now
tell you about the way the Indians
will practice (religion); they will eat Peyote,
or they will Sun Dance; of the two,
which one do you choose?"
"The Sun Dance . . . that's the kind I choose"
said the Young Man, "the Sun Dance.
But my relatives don't practice
any of it" he continued, "they don't
Sun Dance. Of what you describe,
they practice nothing. But I will practice
that kind" he said;

"Now I . . . alright" said Jesus;
"You yourself will be the (Sun Dance) Chief, and I

will then give you the things
with which you'll do it,
what you'll Sun Dance with, what will be done"
He said . . . that's what He told him . . .
so the Young Man agreed, and he did exactly
that way, when he practiced the next summer;
when they did it then,
they just did it for practice,
with only a few people;

the following summer, it was supposed to be
very big, with many people doing it;
and then the Sun Dancers
were to be all dressed up exactly
the same way; the Young Man also had the same outfit,
with an Eagle-Whistle and all, and drums . . .
the way they were going to do it . . .
that's what Jesus told him,
so that's why the Young Man did it (that way);
and when they practiced,
they did it with the singing;

now then, after finishing the practice,
he . . . he, one Indian, an envious one,
came over across, with his hat . . . the center pole
was very, it was very tall;
so he hung his hat up there (on the center pole)
after they had practiced; that person went mad
afterwards, and he ran away;
and lo, his house . . . inside his hat
there was a yellow (cloth) bundle (of bad medicine);
he's the one who put it there;
he was bad-mouthing (the Sun Dance),
he was a bad one,
he did it . . . so he went mad;

then the Young Man . . . Jesus had also

told him: "that . . . don't . . . "
(some people) were bad-mouthing the Young Man
when he practiced the Sun Dance; so then he . . .
when they kept doing that to him, that crowd
spoke ill of him; so later:
"When they speak ill of you,
I myself will (come and) take you
away (to me)" that's what Jesus had told him . . .
"When you have practiced it (the Sun Dance),
I will take you away (to me), if they speak
ill of you, that crowd . . . "

   so then when the Young Man practiced that way,
those people indeed bad-mouthed him;
Jesus had told him (about it) long before that;
at that time He had also told him many
(other) things . . .

   so then the next summer . . .
the next day . . . the next summer when (the Sun Dance)
was supposed to take place,
he died then . . . just . . .
the Young Man died, after they bad-mouthed him;
there were quite a few there when he practiced,
and they all were dressed exactly
the same fine style;
well, there was that woman inside there
where the crowd (of Dancers) was supposed to be,
two women; they were supposed to sit across
(from the Sun Dancers); they weren't supposed
to Sun Dance, only to sit; that's how
it was to be, supposedly;

   and He had also said . . . the Son of
God . . . "You must also do like this,
I tell you" He said;
He told him about everything, about what

will become of everything
on this earth, the way it will happen,
about that, He told him;
The Indian will disappear,
he said, with only a few surviving,
alive; they will have to marry their own kin,
he said then, because they would have become
so few, he said;

　　that's how it is nowadays, just as
he said, with the White-Men becoming
so numerous; they all go to churches;
and (Jesus said that) they'd all
be arguing with each other, all those religions,
He told him; they . . . all over their churches
they would be shooting each other;
that's what has happened now, Jesus told him (about it),
that's what Jesus said . . .

　　I myself often sit and think about it,
knowing all this; I keep thinking,
about that; knowing all this . . .

　　so Jesus told him about everything,
about all that is on this earth; that's how it is,
the way it has become; they even called up
the Indians (to serve) overseas; it has become
that way . . .

　　long time ago . . . that way He . . .
it was long ago . . . there remain other things,
that He also said; this earth
would break open, He said, and the water
would begin to rise, He said;
unless they do the Sun Dance, unless
they run it real good and proper,
unless they run it well;

that Sun Dance is powerful Medicine, (that's)
where the Sun Dancing Indian would get
his Medicine-power; it's that way
that they've come (to have Medicine-Power);
and with it in their hands, like this (gesture),
they would always ward off (bad medicine);
that is, if one does the Sun Dance well,
that's what (Jesus) said, if one does it real well;
that wandering young Ute was to become
a Medicine man;

nowadays I often sit and think about all this;
(about how) they do it the wrong way,
those who do it, those who do
the Sun Dance; it is the wrong way,
it is;

it is Jesus who said it; when I think about it
now . . . there's much more to it, what I
will say, there's much more to it that (Jesus)
had said; there's no end to it,
the way this (the Sun Dance) has become;
He's the one who said that . . . it's Him,
the Son of God; there's much more to it, I myself
know only some of it, I don't know all
of it, I don't remember (all of)
what He said, what He said;
whatever it be, it has become
like that, the way (Jesus) said it,
to him, to the Ute man, it's what He said,
to the Medicine-Man;
I've said it now, this is just about as far as
I know, not very much . . .

Jesus told him this, to him, to the Ute man:
"When you return . . . when you go back home . . .
when you go back, I'll give you one horse"

He told him then; so then later the Young Man
went back, back home . . .
"That horse will catch up with you"
He had told him; "It'll be a black spotted one,
a small one, not very big";
and indeed that happened;

but then he couldn't, when he was going
back home he couldn't catch it;
he came along it four, three (times);
but it kept disappearing that-a-way; and then
afterwards it would come back,
but the Young Man didn't carry anything,

(to catch it with), he didn't have anything,
so wasn't carrying a rope with him,
so he didn't catch it then; he . . .
circling around four times with the horse,
he kept coming up to it
as he was returning home; but he didn't have . . .
anything with which to catch it; that one . . .
that horse . . . that's the one that the Young Man
was supposed to ride
going all over this land;
He had said that, He had told him,
God . . . the Son of God; the Young Man saw Him;
then when he returned home he . . . then . . .
it was like that . . . he didn't catch it,
the horse ran way, that-a-way;
it was supposed to be gentle, the horse,
it was supposed to be a good one;

I sit and think about it, this is the story
they used to tell me,
my long-gone relatives; that's how come
I know it, about how the Sun Dance used to be . . .

. . . so the young man . . . he returned home then,

and he lived on; but later he died;
he is the one who told (his people) about the Sun Dance;
but he did not do it himself;
he died (before that);

    after he died, when he was lying in state,
a rainbow appeared, right above;
and everything was there (on the funeral pyre),
everything, what the Ute man would have worn dancing,
Sun Dancing, it was all there, the bundle
he would have (carried),
his Eagle-Whistle,
what he was supposed to wear, and whatever
else he had; he had done it all properly,
it was like that . . .
he was a real Indian;

    that's what she said . . . she used to tell me this,
my late mother, when she told me stories . . .
I have told it now, where it all
comes from; this is as far as it goes,
what I know.

The Ute name for the Sun Dance, *tagau-wunu-vaci*, means "standing hungry." In this story it is referred to most often as *tagu-nhka-pi* [hunger-dance]. Sometimes it is also referred to simply as *wunu-vaci* [standing]. Some speakers say that the name of the Young Ute man who received the Sun Dance from Jesus was *tuu-naci-too-pu* [Black Cane]. He is said to have been the older brother of Peter Spencer, and thus, the son of a Ute man named *nuu-saaquaci* [Ghost Person].

She-ro-ism

I'm not sure what made me choose writing and teaching as a career. I'm not sure I even chose it. My childhood was full of aloneness, isolation, and the numbing sameness of a mother who both loved and hated routine. She worked to establish and maintain it, then raged against it when she achieved it. I heard those two poles from my room trying to stay out of her way. Knowing whatever I did would bother her. Sometimes doing it anyway. I remember wanting to run, yet having nowhere to go. You know as a child you don't. I remember having a little desk and one book, *Neighbor on the Hill*, which I wanted to write in but was told not to. But I remember making marks somewhere — maybe on my inner thigh. Under my arm. Inside my mouth — on my largest molar. I remember words as something I didn't have. They moved outside the edges of my room. With my pencil I poked holes in the curtains, the window glass, the house itself. Trying to get to the words. I think I would wake sometimes grabbing for them, thinking I held them in my hand, but they were gone. And in school I was unable to speak, unable to perform in any way other than endure. I remember wanting attention. I remember the schoolroom with its high ceilings and teachers also far above me, always out of reach. I was certainly outside their recognition except for their irritation that I was there.

I was other than what they were. I was left out. An invisible erasure that somehow still existed. What was wrong? I still can't say I know. My father and mother were of different backgrounds, different races actually. They married and I was both of neither. Maybe it was neither of both. I was small and dark and somehow unacceptable. I remember the years of self-hating.

I went to college. Married. Had children. Was divorced after nineteen years. I had to earn a living and I could do nothing. I was a writer who was not much published and I finally traveled, teaching creative writing for the State Arts Council of Oklahoma.

But I was born in the heart of the Bible. The Bible Belt that is. And what I had in the middle of it all was the Bible. I went to vacation Bible school. I went to church. Jesus was the Word. Jesus loved the lost sheep. He had a tongue that was a pencil and in the night you were his paper. That's the way I understood it. He gave me his hand moving over my hand showing me how to write until the words I wrote were angels flapping their wings. I had to brush the hair out of my face because they were beating the wind and I had to hold onto the paper too. The whole universe was trying to blow me away but the words kept me there. After those holy visitations, the years followed my car on the road going over and over Oklahoma in stifling classrooms where I faced the stillness, the nothing I remembered in school. But there on the board, the little trail of white that came from the holy chalk like a vapor trail in the prairie sky.

Inside their coats the angels had more words. Stacks and stacks of words. There were words without end. I can't remember how I got the money for my first word processor. It didn't work. A friend, Bud Hollingsworth, sent me my second one. I've had help from friends in the past. And fellowships and grants.

I think it was in 1986, when I was 45, I met Gerald Stern at a writer's conference, as I have said. He recommended me for an Equal Opportunity Fellowship at Iowa. I rented a Ryder truck and a neighbor and a friend helped me load it and I drove from Oklahoma to Iowa City with my cat. I was there for a year when one Sunday afternoon I was sitting in the farmhouse I rented when I got a call from Macalester College in St. Paul. The next fall I commuted between Iowa City and St. Paul to finish my MFA and teach. I was at Macalester six years when I went through a strenuous tenure review that lasted from June, when I handed in my materials, to the following January. I had to present three copies of my books and manuscripts and works-in-progress for outside reviewers. I had to get letters of support from students and colleagues and write my own nine-page single-spaced statement of why I should be considered for tenure. Out of seven going through tenure only three received it. In fact, it was the third week in January before we heard. We were waiting and holding to the thought we would have a job for life or we would have none. All of this on the ice-field of a Minnesota winter. I had even attended the MLA wondering if I should be looking for a job. But now I have tenure and was awarded a year's sabbatical with pay because of some writing projects. I've had a whole year without grading papers, preparing lessons, attending department and faculty and committee meetings of every description when I would much rather be working on my own writing.

I am not a natural teacher. I can't always walk into a classroom talking, but struggle for words to say in class. I struggle for connection to my students. I move in a different place in my head for teaching than I do for writing. I need more time to reach teaching. When I'm discouraged I think that at least teaching is a living because I can't earn it through writing, but that's not true either because I like teaching and want to continue. I teach only five classes a year but that's not as easy as it sounds.

I still have that hunger for words to write — to reach my *neighbor on the hill*. And I can get a lot done. My children are grown and I'm not married and I have that time I used to spend with them. My son is a teacher in Texas and my daughter is an attorney in Missouri. I have a companion also, but he lives his own life, and we meet for dinner. I don't even cook much anymore. My house is small. I clean it myself. I mow my own lawn. Shovel my own walk. I have trouble not letting the house get overrun with papers. Often the dining-room table in my kitchen disappears under them.

Once in a while, I get caught up on my reading for a moment. There's a renaissance in Native American Literature. I go to conferences. I try to organize my house, which I neglected the first six years I was immersed in teaching at Macalester. But mostly I write. Going over it and over it until I don't snag.

When I'm lucky, I read galleys. But mostly, I work. I like experimental writing. A mix of several things together. Fragmented. *Choppied.* I like to make up words to fit the broken disenfranchisement I feel.

I also have stories circulating. And poetry. A file cabinet drawer of poems. May they find their place too. Though I often think—*Nobody wants my work. No one reads me. No one asks me to read. No one comes to my readings. I am no one. Nothing I do matters. I will stay in my room forever. The bats can come and stick to my hair. What does it matter that I've tatooed my whole body with words? That I've tatooed my heart—and inside my head—*

When I feel my failures and the hard edge of frustration over the difficulties of getting published, I also remember the student evaluations that have hurt—to make myself feel worse. One I remember said, "she's a better writer than a teacher." Bless whosever's heart said that. That may seem true when I come into class and I've been working on a story and it's still calling me for attention. Or I've been answering mail and sorting through teaching responsibilities and conference panels and travel arrangements—all competing for my time and attention as though they were children.

Sometimes I have not had my full attention on the class I was teaching. Some times when I cannot give all. Talking about something like using detail in writing, talking about the elements of fiction or poetry, trying to lead a discussion about a story I realize not many have read. And sometimes when I get back to my own poem I can't find again where I was going.

But there're also the flowers I received from a student. I had worked with her on an honor's project and she said, "thanks for your strength and support." There are many students I still hear from. And there are those holy days when classes fly with ease.

I've had a blessed career. I've had a lot published now. At the same time I feel like I still get more rejections than acceptances. But somehow there was an opening in the wall of the house. At least I poked a way through. Surrounded by different worlds moving together simultaneously. I can move through them all. Maybe that's what I found as a child feeling disconnected yet somehow surviving. Remember Jesus my Redeemer and *lamb chop?* I've been able to emerge from silence and the backroads of Oklahoma to a strenuous academic life with many demands, though it took me a long time to know I had a voice and it took me a while to learn to teach.

Sometimes I think of the Ute Sun Dance story. I think of its parts. If a Ute is deer hunting and can't kill a deer — if the Ute is alone — a white man on a white horse appears — before which the white man had been an owl. The white man — who was Jesus — spoke languages until he found the Ute language to speak to the Ute. He said the Devil on a black horse was causing the Ute to feel lonely. Jesus showed the Ute his dead relatives while he was deer hunting and not killing deer. But the Ute was not alone. He had more relatives than he knew. Then Jesus gave a forecast of the mix of American culture — religions of varied interpretations. Jesus said the Ute could choose peyote or the Sun Dance to dance a certain way. The Ute chose to dance. Jesus said he would take him away if anyone laughed. It seems they did. Because the Ute only practiced the Sun Dance and couldn't really do that. And couldn't even catch the small black spotted horse Jesus gave him. The horse was robust and the Ute didn't have any rope to catch it with. Couldn't seem to do anything in the story. But the horse was there anyway. And the rainbow appeared over the Ute's funeral pyre. The eagle-whistle and bundle he would have carried. Despite his shortcomings, the Ute died significantly. In the long cold winter of the Sun Dance where he lived.

Sometimes I feel I deal with personal mediocrity and failure and staying on top of the demanding, every-minute work at school without ever having it all *zippied up*. I think of the students who have kept books I loaned them. Students who never gave of themselves in class. I still deal with the feelings of marginality. In my dark moods I still feel unacceptable. Yet I know the center of being when I'm writing something I like — or when class discussions go as they should — and you feel exhilaration from teaching the rest of the day. Sometimes I get stomped on — yet I go on. I know the poles of strength and discouragement. I know them often. My polarities are different than my mother's, yet I have them too.

But I woke up this morning and picked up my pencil and began writing. Here in my writing room where I face the wolves and know I am a sheep but the shepherd is there you better believe it and I have come through the prairie and I have come through the wind that could erase the toes from your feet and I have novels and short stories and poetry and essays and plays that I send out and get back and I will keep on because it's my survival. My life. I write through the *aloneness* that fills the house much as it did when I was a girl hitting my pencil to find a hole. A way through.

A Fieldbook of Textual Migrations

Ta pollai teileafoin
ag bagairt orm.
[Telephone poles threaten me.]
Nuala ni Dhomhnaill, Maidin sa
Domhan Toir [Oriental Morning]

I.

In a Field Where Meanings *Quantitate*

I do not speak Cherokee, but when I read the language, I see the *spaciness* of words to make meaning. To stretch across the possibilities of what could be said. Not limiting it.

The telephone, for instance: *di-tla-no-he?-di-(i)*. They (words) made of (or placed on) the wind (or air) have been brought to one place to be used.

That descriptive noun, which contains verbs and other parts of speech, makes the telephone familiar. It uses the natural elements of wind (or air). The old ways are embedded in technology. The same principles of trust and reciprocity hold. The conduits still connect.

In another instance of the roominess in the Cherokee language, I read a sentence that assures that artificial lights work as well as natural light: *di-gi'-ga-ge a-le di-tse-yu:-s-d(i) da:-gi-(ha) di-tsv'-s-di*. I have some red and green lights. Or, plural-nonliving-red and plural-nonliving-green them I-of-indefinite-shape have nonliving to be turned on with. (Taking several lines in English to say what can be said in Cherokee in one.)

In general (though Indian languages are different) Indian languages are often an abstraction of the pragmatic. An arrangement of words that makes them heard in different directions. A migration of *making it said*. Of it being heard.

tsu'-tla ni-ga-we:-s-gv ga-tv'-gi?-(a). Fox just spoke it I am hearing. The fox just spoke *it*. *It* I am hearing. The one *it* ties the two participants together. You see the language does what it also is doing. It is spoken for grouping. A reciprocal reciprocity.

ha'-l(i)-s-du-tlv'-ga. Bend yourself on something.

i-da-nv'-ni-da. Let's be sitting around.

That's what it is to make an easement. To share a place where *talking* can happen. For the purpose of *refielding*. For understanding. For making the adjustments that survival adjusts.

2.

A Field Where a Heritage Is Split

What do you do with a mixed-blood heritage other than being a sitting duck in the water for those who want to expel your voice from what they consider their boat?

I grew up in my mother's white family. I felt my difference every day.

If I say I am an Indian part, what do I do with the white? And what do I do with the hollowness where the Cherokee language should have been?

I can say I remember the sound of something *like wind coming out from both sides of the tongue (thlu)*. I remember the way my father said double *ll*'s (such as *million*). The way the word *flapped* in his mouth.

I remember something like *go whay la* or *doe dah gah ho*.

But the sound of language in my ear is English. What I have from the Cherokee is the possibilities of meaning. The arrangements of thought.

I know instead of separate words there are clumps of words that connect in different ways. I know Cherokee words are spoken differently on different occasions. And the spelling of words is up to the one who is spelling.

3.

Locations

As if Columbus arriving to America.
There were inhabitants on the land
but they could be unthorned.

The Pilgrims could establish
their own centeredness they could claim
as theirs what is already inhabited
as though it hadn't.

They came with their cavalry maneuvers of language. They dislodged the lodgepoles of Indian languages. They dismantled meanings from a continent.

It was their disruption of languages.

It is to be Indian. To be dewinged. As if deplaned. Just when you think you're going somewhere.

To be Indian is to know the loss of language. It is a longing for that moveability. For the words stranded from their strandedness. (Stranded as in yarn. Not stranded by itself until someone comes.)

To lose words that serve as a *functional*. To be *delanguaged* is a *recitrocity*. It has ramifications.

If English itself is a stretchy language, as I have heard, imagine what it would have been with the otherness of the languages it met. Without the *interfuss* of them. Which is their absence.

Without them, the doors of connections to other possibilities are tightly shut. *s-da-ya da-s-du-ha di-s-du?-di*, which is said by saying, *closely closed closers*.

The placement of English on the continent was a four-pronged caltrop. No matter how it was placed on the ground, one prong always stuck up. To prevent the walking of cattle or horses.

Those who came brought their pronged instruments to stick in the hoof or in the mouth.

Putting the languages into the English Melting Pot. I was through school before they took out of the pot. What clumped that wasn't stirred because it was the continent's bedrock.

To know there would not be an idea that would hold *tow rope*. And I am now in a field-pond with an *insect* of voices.

Language is the consciousness of the one who speaks it.

As though America were the place Columbus came. The Pilgrims and emigrants and settlers following. With their *referations* and *terminates*.

I could put English into the Indian melting pot. Make my attack on syntax. Spell in my own way. Use malappropriate words. Invent the theory of *fluxativity*.

4.

In a Field of Indian Languages
Doors inside a Corridor
the Corridor inside an Entry Way
the Entry Way inside a Room
the Room inside a Museum

At the Weisman Art Museum, University of Minnesota, I saw a mixed media construction called *Pedicord Apartments*, by Edward and Nancy Kienholz, 1985.

It was an actual apartment entry hall that had been taken out of its place and displayed in the museum. Inside the entry hall, there was an adjacent corridor with six doors, three on each side. As you walked into the hallway and stood at the doors, you could hear the sounds behind them. A television. A barking dog. A woman crying. A conversation. Silence. No one home?

As I stood at the last door, I thought I heard something barely brush the door on the other side. I couldn't be sure, but I was momentarily alarmed. What if the door suddenly opened? Was this mixed media construction a confrontation with some revelation of the self? I questioned what I was doing. I wanted to leave. What if I were caught listening? I was aware I was eavesdropping, even though rooms weren't actually on the other side of the doors. Even though I had to eavesdrop before I could hear, which was part of the construction.

It threw the real upon me. I had consciousness of myself and the act I was committing. Even though it was only a construct of mostly what was imagined. The hearer filled in the missing part, made a connection to what wasn't.

An entrapment? As tenement living is? A partial of the actual? Untenable? A told-to-stay-there: *ka-no-hu-yu-hi*, a reservation?

Sometimes I am doing something in my house and someplace else comes to mind and superimposes itself over what I'm doing though it seems to have no apparent relationship. As though it were the reality going on and what I was actually doing was trapped in the memory of a place I had been years ago.

Something like that is what an Indian (Cherokee) language is.

5.

to-tsu'-hwa, the Cardinal

As though I stand at the old language and listen.

Tsi'-s-qua u-ga'-no-wv da-yu'-ni-lo:-sv a-ni-no-hi-lo:-ga. Birds south from coming on their way are flying.

You think the bits of paper she brings
from the bakery would hold water,
the nest like a half globe in the branch.

Is she building a bowl in which her eggs will float?

Does she think the earth will open?

And a flood will carry off her language unless she teaches them?

6.

Over Who Will Reign Chief of Words

Indian languages (in general) speak in an other.

A *poetrix* of language.

They are gathered, beloved.

The Pilgrim fathers. The *reservests*. They came to worship. They didn't know how close.

I-tse Ka-no-ge:-dv Da-tlo-hi-s-tv. New Pronouncements as He Went About. That's the way to say the New Testament in Cherokee. The *spaciness*. The adaptability ongoing. More than making it up as you go.

There is a written language that was invented on this continent. A little burst of something unnoticed. An alphabet that is a syllabary, which is a letter for each syllable, because Cherokee syllables end in vowels. *di-tla-no-he?-di-(i)* [the telephone]. But it is a whole language written here and now, rather than over centuries and continents, like English.

I have a visage of that burst. That blast. That vent. I'm going to town now. I can separate one letter from another. Or parts of words from the others. So that in con(found)ing there is a *found* separate from the *con* and the *ing* at the start and finish of the word. It is the

Cherokee influence of knowing how many things can mean. When one is confused, there is always an understanding of something imbedded within it. Even if it is not always the understanding of what you wanted to understand.

It's what it's like to write words I can't speak. I have to say them in something other than they are. Because directly is not a route.

As if I said there is a God because there is language.

But that language was crucified.

After the *cavalry of calvary*, the Cherokee language was put on the cross and nailed and *tombed* away and the next day, *rebold*. The *tone* was moved away. The whole grass mowed and the new day rumbled, *it is risen*.

It is gone for me, as far away as if in heaven, but it's life is in the thoughts behind my words.

Acknowledgment to *Beginning Cherokee*, 2d ed., by Ruth Bradley Holmes and Betty Sharp Smith (Norman: University of Oklahoma Press, 1977).

Newmerica

1.

The antlers on my church are steeples in the woods of religion's regionalism (is from where I'm from).

E(van)gelical America brought north with me in a (moving) van.

2.

A red house.

A field behind. Not the one there now, but the one when I was a girl, which is not there anymore, having been built upon by the building where cars swarm Sunday like insects.

If I could not look back. If I could go on.

Even then, I could say to the sky's insections, *behold*.

Behold was my favorite word.

Behold he comes in (glo)ry.

3.

When a church sits on my head. Is there a while.

A corner grocer.

A closet in a room.

A land called church within a church
within another church within another.

A corral beside a red barn.

A barn beside a field.

The squeak of brakes arriving
all airy

all noisy as someone eating
a church supper.

4.

 I would not want to be like Mary. I would not want to hear Jesus
ask for milk.

5.

 As long as the finger never ended
Pinocchio was a childhood story.
 Not a lie to tell anyone.
 How did I know it was not a lie?
 Because it was the same story told twice in a different way.

 There it went fifteen feet long again
pulling down the face with its weight
as the earth made trips around the sun
and the sun around the spread feet of the quarter moon.
 Somehow we become more than we are.

6.

 I wanted to suffer with Christ.
 He was the motor vehicle. The numerical license plate. I could look
up at the ceiling of my small room and think I heard Christ tapping
a message. He was asking me to see how he'd suffered on the cross. I
said I'd been to the Sun Dance. I'd seen them drag buffalo skulls on
a rope with skewers piercing their back. The suffering they did was for
him. I told him I knew it was hard to get in the room he called light.
 I fasted and wept.
 I prayed until I knew heaven was a thought.

7.

 I prayed until I knew thought was a heaven.
 A sacred place in the landscape of the mind.
 The act of the will in a landscape of survival.
 A script of thought.

A meaning to follow.
Somewhere there.
An opening to the new millenium of the new world which was
actually the old world the new world thought it came to
  moving toward an open end
  an upward spiral without a cap
  there would be no stopping it
  riding to shore holding to a board from a broken ship
  for a cold-and-hunger dance.

Bibliography

Novels

Flutie. Wakefield, RI: Moyer Bell, 1998.
The Only Piece of Furniture in the House. Wakefield, RI: Moyer Bell, 1996.
Pushing the Bear. New York: Harcourt Brace, 1996.

Short Stories

Monkey Secret. Evanston, IL: Northwestern University Press, 1995.
Firesticks. Norman: University of Oklahoma Press, 1993.
Trigger Dance. Normal: Illinois State University Fiction Collective Two, 1990. Published in German under the title *Tante Parnettas Elektrische Wunden*, trans. Alissa Walser (Frankfurt: S. Fischer Verlag, 1995).

Essays

The West Pole. Minneapolis: University of Minnesota Press, 1997.
Claiming Breath. Lincoln: University of Nebraska Press, 1992.

Poetry

Boom Town. Goodhue, MN: Black Hat Press, 1995.
Coyote's Quodlibet. Tucson: Chax Press, 1995.
Lone Dog's Winter Count. Albuquerque: West End Press, 1991.
Iron Woman. Minneapolis: New Rivers Press, 1990.
Offering. Duluth: Holy Cow! Press, 1988.
One Age in a Dream. Minneapolis: Milkweed Editions, 1986.

Drama

War Cries. Duluth: Holy Cow! Press, 1996.